ITIL® 4 – A

CW00541689

## Other publications by Van Haren Publishing

Van Haren Publishing (VHP) specializes in titles on Best Practices, methods and standards within four domains:
- IT and IT Management
- Architecture (Enterprise and IT)
- Business Management and
- Project Management

Van Haren Publishing is also publishing on behalf of leading organizations and companies: ASLBiSL Foundation, BRMI, CA, Centre Henri Tudor, Gaming Works, IACCM, IAOP, IFDC, Innovation Value Institute, IPMA-NL, ITSqc, NAF, KNVI, PMI-NL, PON, The Open Group, The SOX Institute.

Topics are (per domain):

| IT and IT Management | Enterprise Architecture | Project Management |
|---|---|---|
| ABC of ICT | ArchiMate® | A4-Projectmanagement |
| ASL® | GEA® | DSDM/Atern |
| CATS CM® | Novius Architectuur | ICB / NCB |
| CMMI® | Methode | ISO 21500 |
| COBIT® | TOGAF® | MINCE® |
| e-CF | | M_o_R® |
| ISO/IEC 20000 | **Business Management** | MSP® |
| ISO/IEC 27001/27002 | BABOK® Guide | P3O® |
| ISPL | BiSL® and BiSL® Next | PMBOK® Guide |
| IT4IT® | BRMBOK™ | Praxis® |
| IT-CMF™ | BTF | PRINCE2® |
| IT Service CMM | EFQM | |
| ITIL® | eSCM | |
| MOF | IACCM | |
| MSF | ISA-95 | |
| SABSA | ISO 9000/9001 | |
| SAF | OPBOK | |
| SIAM™ | SixSigma | |
| TRIM | SOX | |
| VeriSM™ | SqEME® | |

For the latest information on VHP publications, visit our website: www.vanharen.net.

# ITIL® 4

## A Pocket Guide

Jan van Bon

# Colophon

| | |
|---|---|
| Title: | ITIL® 4 – A Pocket Guide |
| Author: | Jan van Bon |
| Publisher: | Van Haren Publishing, 's-Hertogenbosch, www.vanharen.net |
| Design & layout: | Coco Bookmedia, Amersfoort-NL |
| ISBN Hardcopy: | 978 94 018 0439 4 |
| ISBN eBook (pdf): | 978 94 018 0440 0 |
| ISBN EPUB: | 978 94 018 0441 7 |
| Edition: | First edition, first impression, April 2019 |

# Foreword

This pocket guide delivers a concise summary of ITIL 4, published in 2019. It is based on the ITIL® Foundation, ITIL 4 edition and the associated training instructions, providing the ultimate fit in terms of preparing for the ITIL 4 Foundation exam. If you're not preparing for the exam, it offers a quick reference to the basic concepts of ITIL 4.

This pocket guide will provide readers with an awareness of the ITIL 4 service management framework, by understanding:

- the key concepts of service management
- how the seven ITIL guiding principles can help an organization adopt and adapt service management
- the four dimensions of service management
- the purpose and components of the ITIL service value system
- the six activities of the service value chain, and how they interconnect
- the purpose and key terms of 15 of the 34 ITIL practices
- seven of these 15 ITIL practices in detail

All requirements for the ITIL 4 Foundation exam are covered in this pocket guide. Chapter 6 describes these requirements. The pocket guide delivers all information on the material you need to know at Blooms level 1 (recall/define) together with the material you need to understand at Blooms level 2 (describe/explain). Please note that this pocket guide represents the content of the ITIL 4 Foundation Exam Specification of January 2019. If any new version is subsequently released after that date, students should study the differences.

It also provides support for anyone who has knowledge of previous ITIL editions and is looking for a bridge to the new edition. ITIL 4 took a big leap into the modern world of IT service management, covering the latest principles and practices in a customer-focused, service-centric way, enabling Agile principles for the maximum support of any business.

If you want to use this pocket guide as a preparation for the ITIL 4 Foundation exam, please focus on the standard (black) text. All content that is beyond the basic exam requirements is formatted in a different way, as slightly colored text (*as in this paragraph*) This will support you even more in using this pocket guide in your preparations for the exam.

I'm convinced that this pocket guide will provide an excellent reference tool for practitioners, students and others who want a concise summary of the key ITIL 4 concepts.

# Acknowledgements

Following the official publication of ITIL 4, this pocket guide was developed as an update of the well-known ITIL V2 and V3 pocket guides, produced by the same editors.

The text of this pocket guide was reviewed by a team of experts in the domain of IT service management and ITIL. The integrated Review Team was composed of the following experts:
- Maarten Bordewijk (Bordewijk Training & Advies, NL)
- John Deland (ITSM Consultant, Canada)
- Frederik van Eeden (Erik van Eeden, NL)
- Jaap Germans (Pink Elephant, NL)
- Peter van Gijn (CGI, NL)
- Jan Heunks (Management Consulting Solutions, NL)
- Kevin Holland (independent, UK)
- Matiss Horodishtiano (independent, Israel)
- Karel Höster (Global Knowledge, NL)
- Steve Mann (SM2 Ltd, UK)
- Roman Zhuravlev (AXELOS)

All reviewers spent their valuable hours on a detailed review of the text, answering the core question, "Is the content of this pocket guide a correct reflection of the core content of ITIL 4 and does it cover the ITIL 4 Foundation exam requirements, given the limited size of a pocket guide?"

Providing several hundred valuable improvement issues, they contributed significantly to the quality of this pocket guide, and we thank them for that.

# Contents

## 6 THE ITIL 4 FOUNDATION EXAM ................................... 99

# The ITIL story

ITIL has been the leading guidance for IT service management over the past three decades. Millions of practitioners worldwide have applied its guidance in their daily jobs, providing a structured approach to one of the most important support domains for modern business: the provision of information technology services for the improvement of business results.

In the modern digital business, the role of information technology (IT) has further increased and it has merged with many other domains. This emphasizes the role of IT even more. And with the acceleration of business change, IT itself needs to change even faster to support the business that it has merged with. This means that the IT service provider will have to apply Agile ways of delivering its contribution to the co-creation of value. In other words: it was time for a new edition of ITIL guidance.

In the first version of ITIL, from the end of the 1980's up to the turn of the century, the guidance was based on a long list of best practices that were documented in dozens of small books. Although the exact number of books is under some debate, the total library counted some 50 titles. This guidance largely focused on the support of technology.

In 2000-2001 the ITIL guidance was updated and documented in a set of two core books: ITIL Service Support and ITIL Service Delivery. In the following years, additional guidance was published, but the two core books remained the authoritative references.

In 2007, the third version of ITIL was published: ITIL v3. It was built on the paradigm of a Service Lifecycle with five phases, and each phase was documented in a separate publication. These five core books were then updated in 2011 in a minor review of ITIL v3, with few differences. The ITIL v3 editions changed the focus from technology to services.

The pace of development in the IT industry in the last decade accelerated in such a way that a thoroughly redefined version of ITIL was required. It was not only technology and the role of IT in business that had made huge progress, but the practices used in the IT industry had also gone through some serious evolution, with Agile and DevOps approaches, cloud technology, and the merging of IT with many other domains being some of the most prominent features.

With the new ITIL 4, a major step has been taken to cover the latest developments. The ITIL 4 guidance supports modern ways of co-creating value in an active collaboration of stakeholders, using an Agile approach in a customer-focused setting. Its holistic approach not only underpins the management of IT services, but now also supports other domains, enabling the integration of IT with the business and with other support domains.

# **1** Introduction

Learning outcomes:
- Understand the purpose and components of the ITIL service value system.

Assessment criteria:
- Describe the ITIL service value system

The past decade has illustrated that delivering services has become the mainstream economic model. The merging of IT and business, and the increasing pace of development of technology, has created the need for a fully-fledged, strategic IT service management capability.

The digitization of companies and economies has made it clear that organizations must learn to deliver their IT-enabled services in a flexible way, combining Agile approaches with guarantees for predictability and stability. This places significant responsibility on the shoulders of IT service management and on its leading guidance, ITIL.

ITIL has provided leading guidance for IT service management for more than 30 years. ITIL 4 brings ITIL up-to-date by re-shaping much of the established practices in the wider context of customer experience, value streams, and digital transformation, as well as embracing new approaches such as Lean, Agile, and DevOps.

# ■ 1.1   THE ITIL 4 FRAMEWORK

The key components of the ITIL 4 framework are the ITIL service value
system (SVS) and the four dimensions model.

## 1.1.1   The ITIL service value system (SVS)

The **ITIL service value system** (SVS) is a model demonstrating how all the
components and activities of an organization work together to facilitate
value creation through IT-enabled services.

*[handwritten: System- wide thing]*
*[handwritten: Chain - Central core, p45]*

These components of the SVS include:

- the ITIL service value chain
- the ITIL practices
- the ITIL guiding principles
- governance
- continual improvement

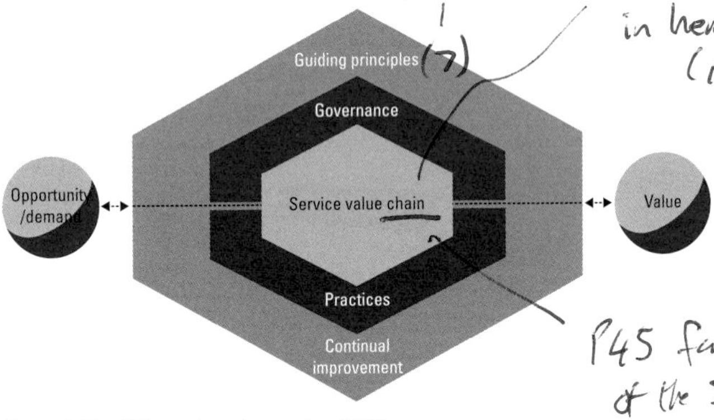

*[handwritten: Patterns of Value streams in here! (p37)]*
*[handwritten: p41]*

Figure 1.  The ITIL service value system (SVS)

*[handwritten: P45 for details of the S.V. chain]*

The **ITIL service value chain** is a set of interconnected activities that an
organization performs in order to deliver a valuable product or service to
its consumers and to facilitate value realization. It provides an operating

model for service providers that covers six key activities, applying practices to continually improve the enabled values.

The **ITIL practices** are sets of organizational resources designed for performing work or accomplishing an objective. Activities in the service value chain can be based on established practices.

The **ITIL guiding principles** are recommendations that can guide an organization in all circumstances, regardless of changes in its goals, strategies, type of work, or management structure. The ITIL guiding principles assure that the organization performs in a consistent, effective and efficient way.

**Governance** is the means by which an organization is directed and controlled. The organization's governance is based on a consistent set of guiding principles. Governance enables the organization to ensure that its operations are always aligned with its strategy.

**Continual improvement** is a recurring organizational activity performed at all levels to ensure that an organization's performance continually meets stakeholders' expectations.

Using all these components, the service provider can continually improve its services. Continual improvement is a core component of the SVS, as in previous versions of ITIL guidance. It is based on the continual improvement model (Figure 10) and supported by various ITIL practices.

### 1.1.2 The four dimensions model
In a holistic approach, ITIL 4 covers all four dimensions required for the effective and efficient facilitation of value for customers and other

stakeholders in the form of products and services. The SVS should be considered from all of these four dimensions:

- organizations and people
- information and technology
- partners and suppliers
- value streams and processes

These four dimensions should be managed in an integrated way, balancing their contribution to an effective SVS. The four dimensions are described in more detail in chapter 3.

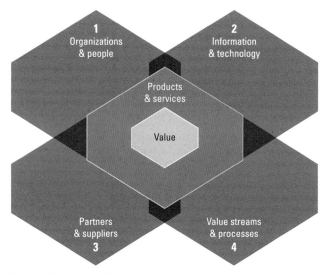

Figure 2. The four dimensions of service management

# 2 Key concepts of service management

Before describing how ITIL supports organizations to continually improve services and co-create value, the definitions of service management and value need to be clear.

> **Service management**: A set of specialized organizational capabilities for enabling value for customers in the form of services.

The purpose of an organization is to create value for its stakeholders.

> **Value**: The perceived benefits, usefulness and importance of something.

This introduces the following questions:

■ What is the nature of value?
■ What is the nature and scope of the stakeholders involved?
■ How is value creation enabled through services?

## ■ 2.1 VALUE CO-CREATION

Value can be subjective: the value is determined by the stakeholders.

Organizations increasingly recognize that value is co-created through an active collaboration between stakeholders, including the service providers and service consumers. Each stakeholder receives its own value in the interaction. The relationship between service provider and service consumer is mutually beneficial. An effective service value chain requires collaboration between providers and consumers.

After many years of focusing on operational excellence, the era of customer-focused service excellence has now arrived. Service delivery is increasingly becoming the core element in the economy. People are buying less and less 'pure' goods, and suppliers are increasingly packaging supplied goods into a service offering. The support that comes with that service has already revealed itself as a dominant differentiator for the success of organizations. This observation applies to both internal and external services.

In the economy this shift is indicated with Service-Dominant logic (S-D logic), as a successor to the Goods-Dominant logic (G-D logic) in which the transfer of goods played the main role. According to the S-D logic, service is the fundamental basis for all value-sharing[1].

---

1    [Ref.: Service-dominant logic 2025]

G-D logic focuses on value creation in the transfer of goods (value-in-exchange). S-D logic focuses on value creation in the use of resources (value-in-use), where value is co-created by providers and consumers.

## ◼ 2.2 STAKEHOLDERS

There are various stakeholders involved in the co-creation of value: service providers, service consumers, and others. The ITIL 4 guidance is applied to the way *organizations* can improve their contribution.

> *Organization*: A person or a group of people that has its own functions with responsibilities, authorities, and relationships to achieve its objectives.

An organization can be anything, ranging from a single individual or team, up to a complex set of organizational structures in a network.

### 2.2.1 Service providers

**Service provider** is a role performed by an organization in a service relationship to provide services to consumers. A service provider co-creates value with the consumer, by offering services.

Service providers can be external or internal to the consumer's organization. An internal service provider is part of the same organization as the consumer. External providers often provide their services as a commercial offering to various consumers. The provider-consumer model can be applied to create complex supply chains, service networks, or service ecosystems.

A service provider needs to have a clear understanding of who its consumers are.

### 2.2.2 Service consumers

When receiving services, an organization takes on the generic role of the **service consumer**. Service consumers collaborate with service providers in the co-creation of value.

For the generic role of service consumer, ITIL 4 makes a distinction between three separate roles: customer, user and sponsor.

*Defines*

*Uses*

*Pay!*

> **Customer**: A person who defines the requirements for a service and takes responsibility for the outcomes of service consumption.
>
> **User**: A person who uses services.
>
> **Sponsor**: A person who authorizes budget for service consumption.

These roles can be used in any combination. In any service relationship it is important that these roles are fully identified, as this will assist with communications and the management of stakeholders. Each role could have different expectations of the services and the expected value from them.

### 2.2.3 Other stakeholders

There can be many other stakeholders that play a role in value creation:

- **Shareholders** are interested in the success of the organization, often in terms of financial benefits.
- **Employees** of the service provider may be interested in other value, including professional growth, financial compensation and sense of purpose.
- The **community** may have relations with the services. This may cover charity, environmental factors, employment, social impact, etc.

# ■ 2.3   PRODUCTS AND SERVICES

> *Service*: *A means of enabling <u>value co-creation</u> by facilitating outcomes that customers want to achieve, without the customer having to manage specific costs and risks.*

Services are based on one or more products.

> *Product*: *A configuration of an organization's resources designed to offer value for a consumer.*

The organization's resources include the four dimensions of service management: organizations and people, information and technology, partners and suppliers, value streams and processes. The service provider enables access to these resources, to be used by the consumer in such a way that these resources are valuable to the consumer. Goods may be transferred to the consumer as part of the service.

Products may not be exclusive to consumer groups: they can be used for different purposes and for different consumer groups.

Products are usually only partially visible to the consumer.
E.g., a network provision can be part of the offered product, but consumers will not be able to see the network itself, they will only be able to use it for their own purposes.

## 2.3.1   Service offerings

A service provider and a consumer can agree on services that are offered by the service provider.

> *Service offering*: *A formal description of one or more services, designed to address the needs of a target consumer group.*

A service offering may include:

- a wide variety of **goods** (e.g. a laptop), to be supplied to a consumer
- **access to resources** (e.g. a network or storage, possibly through a laptop), granted or licensed to a consumer under agreed terms and conditions *e.g. access to a mobile phone network.*
- **service actions** (e.g. user support), performed to address a consumer's needs

The service offering is often demonstrated to consumers in the format of a **service catalogue**.

Services are offered to target consumer groups, internal or external to the service provider organization. The service provider is responsible for the resources made available to the consumer, goods to be supplied, and service actions to be performed.

## ■ 2.4   SERVICE RELATIONSHIPS

Any and all organizations are both service provider and service consumer. An organization will assume the role of provider or consumer within the context of a given relationship with another organization.

When provisioning services, an organization takes on the role of the service provider. The provider can be external to the consumer's organization, or they can both be part of the same organization.

> **Service provision**: Activities performed by an organization to provide services.

The service provider:

- manages the **resources** that are *configured* to deliver the service
- provides **access** to these resources for users
- fulfils the **agreed service actions** (support)

Service provision may also include the supplying of **goods**.

The service provider will also have to manage the service performance (*service level management*), and to *continually improve* the services provided, to maintain the relationship and the value (co-)created.

The consumer consumes the services provided by the service provider.

> **Service consumption**: *Activities performed by an organization to consume services.*

The consumer:
- manages its **own resources** that are needed to use the service
- performs **service actions**, including **utilizing the provider's resources**, and requesting service actions to be fulfilled

The consumer may also receive (acquire) **goods**, delivered by the provider as parts of the service.

Service providers and service consumers have a relationship, based on the services provided by the provider to the consumer. This leads to a service relationship between providers and consumers.

> **Service relationship**: *A cooperation between a service provider and service consumer, including service provision, service consumption, and service relationship management.*

This relationship needs to be managed.

> **Service relationship management**: *Joint activities performed by a service provider and a service consumer to ensure continual value co-creation based on agreed and available service offerings.*

These activities include regular meetings over the delivered services, discussing new options, preparing for future needs, adjusting the service level agreements/contracts, etc. In business-to-consumer services, this may include surveys and other marketing research.

### 2.4.1  The service relationship model

The basic unit of one provider and one consumer can be repeated over and over again, to create endless chains and networks of provider-consumer relationships. For each unit, the provider creates new resources for the consumer or modifies existing resources.

In these service ecosystems, the term provider indicates a *relative* position: each consumer on its turn is a provider when that consumer adds value to the received services and provides it to the next position in the chain or network. This way, complex ecosystems of provider-consumer relationships can be created (Figure 3).

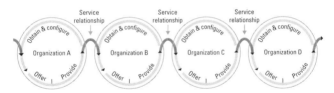

Figure 3.  The service relationship model

## ■ 2.5  VALUE

Value is co-created in a service relationship between service consumer and service provider, as well as other stakeholders that are part of the relevant service relationship.

Value is only achieved when relationships have more positive effects than negative. This is a balance between desired outcomes and the associated costs and risks.

From the consumer's perspective a service represents potential value, in terms of potential benefits at given costs and risks. On the one hand, the consumer has to define these benefits. Benefits can relate to gains created and/or pains relieved[2]. On the other hand, the consumer has to define the financial costs of the service (costs of service, risks imposed, etc.). A positive balance will lead to a service relationship with the service provider.

The relationship between the service and the desired outcomes is expressed in terms of the utility and warranty of the service.

### 2.5.1  Outcomes

The direct result of an activity is an output.

> **Output**: A tangible or intangible deliverable of an activity.

Outcomes result from the use of these outputs (see Figure 6). The service provider produces outputs that help its consumers to achieve these outcomes.

> **Outcome**: A result for a stakeholder enabled by one or more outputs.

To a large extent outcomes determine the actual value for the consumer. And as value is determined by the consumer, outcomes should also be determined by the consumer.

Service providers should spend serious amounts of effort in understanding the nature of the consumer's needs and business characteristics, so that they are able to contribute to the desired outcomes for the consumer.

---

2    [Ref.: Value Proposition Design]

## 2.5.2 Costs

The co-creation of value often involves a transfer of money from the consumer to the provider. This is income for the provider, and cost for the consumer.

> *Cost*: The amount of money spent on a specific activity or resource.

Often, costs are financial, but they may also be expressed in non-financial ways, e.g. as time that is spent or avoided by resources. Ultimately, all costs can be expressed in terms of money, so they can be compared and used in a business case for the service consumer, weighing *costs removed* and *costs imposed*:

- A service may **remove costs** from the service consumer: reduced costs of staff, technology, and other resources, which the consumer does not need to provide any more.
- A service may also **impose costs** on the service customer: a price may be charged by the service provider, and there are other costs such as staff training, costs of network utilization, procurement, etc., which come with the service.

## 2.5.3 Risks

A service may also introduce new risks imposed on the service consumer, resulting from using the service.

> *Risk*:
> 1. A possible event that could cause harm or loss, or make it more difficult to achieve objectives.
> 2. Uncertainty of outcome that can be used in the context of measuring the probability of positive outcomes as well as negative outcomes.

From the customer's perspective, as with costs, risks can be removed as well as imposed. The consumer should weigh *risks removed* and *risks imposed* in the business case of the service proposition:

- A service may **remove risks** from the service consumer: failure of the consumer's infrastructure or lack of consumer's staff will be avoided (or mitigated), through the use of the service provider's more reliable resources.
- A service may **impose risks** on the service consumer: the provider's resources may fail or experience security breaches.

These risks need to be balanced with the net result of costs removed and costs imposed. This requires the customer *and* the provider to both clearly understand the impact of the service on the user's business. The consumer contributes to this by clearly articulating the service requirements and its desired outcomes, defining the associated critical success factors (CSFs) and constraints. The service provider and the service consumer cooperate in the management of risks, balancing their interests.

*service consumer participates in setting requirements, reducing risks*

The provider should also have access to the necessary resources of the consumer during the service relationship.

### 2.5.4 Utility and warranty

The evaluation of the ability of a service to provide the desired outcomes requires an assessment of the utility and warranty of the service. Both utility and warranty are essential to the creation of value.

*Utility*: The functionality offered by a product or service to meet a particular need.

*What it does*

Utility can be summarized as 'what the service does' and can be used to determine whether a service is '*fit for purpose*'. This requires that a service either supports the business activities of the consumer or removes constraints from the consumer - or both.

*Warranty*: The assurance that a product or service will meet agreed requirements.

*Does it do it?*

Warranty relates to how the service performs: is it '*fit for use*'? Like for utility, this can be expressed in terms of **service levels** that should be agreed and aligned with the needs of consumers, including:

- availability
- capacity
- security
- continuity

A service may be said to provide acceptable assurance, or *warranty*, if all defined and agreed conditions are met.

# 3 The four dimensions of service management

Learning outcome:
- ✓ Understand the four dimensions of service management.

Assessment criteria:
- ✓ Describe the four dimensions of service management: organizations and people, information and technology, partners and suppliers, value streams and processes.

There are four dimensions required for designing and delivering services (as shown in Figure 4). Each of these four dimensions represents a *perspective*, used for a holistic approach to service management:

1. organizations and people
2. information and technology
3. partners and suppliers
4. value streams and processes

*POPIT, plus partners and suppliers*

The represented perspectives are relevant to the whole SVS, including the service value chain and all ITIL practices. A holistic approach requires all four dimensions to be addressed in service management initiatives. The dimensions may overlap to some extent: there are no sharp boundaries.

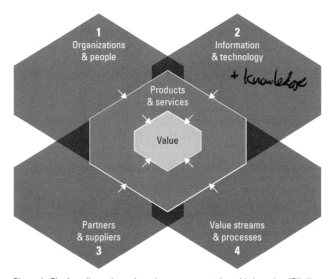

Figure 4. The four dimensions of service management (graphic based on ITIL 4)

## ■ 3.1   ORGANIZATIONS AND PEOPLE

The organizations and people dimension of a service covers roles and responsibilities, organizational structures, culture, and skills and competencies of staff, all of which are required to conduct the activities of the service provider.

The availability and competence of workforce by themselves are not sufficient. The organization also needs to make sure there is an adequate culture that enables continual improvement across the organization. Culture covers various perspectives, including:

■ shared values and attitudes

■ leaders who champion and advocate these values

- communication between various stakeholders
- trust and transparency

Aspects to be covered in the organizations and people dimension include:
- management and leadership styles
- skills and competencies
- communication and collaboration
- T-shaped individuals, covering broad knowledge combined with a deep specialization[3]
- common objectives and goals
- collaboration with other teams, breaking down silos

The organizations and people dimension relates to the SVS, covering the following aspects:
- roles and responsibilities
- formal organizational structure
- organizational culture
- required staffing and competencies

These aspects relate to creating, improving and delivering services and they need to be addressed when managing and improving the SVS at all levels.

## ■ 3.2   INFORMATION AND TECHNOLOGY

The technology applied by service providers covers two types. First, it covers the technology elements in the service, used by the consumer. In IT services this can include applications, networks, databases, cloud computing etc.

---

3    Alternatives are Pi-shaped individuals who have two adjacent fields of expertise, I-shaped individuals who do not possess a broad knowledge, and generalists who are commonly referred to as Dash-shaped people. [Ref.: A Primer on the T-professional, 2017]

The technology also encompasses the internal technological infrastructure that is required to *manage* these IT products. This second type of technology includes workflow management tooling, communication systems, knowledge bases, a configuration management database (CMDB) and inventory systems, cloud solutions, and many more.

> **Cloud computing**: A model for enabling on-demand network access to a shared pool of configurable computing resources that can be rapidly provided with minimal management effort or provider interaction.

Architecture specifies how the technology should be selected and designed. The skills required to manage the technology should be available from within the service provider's staff. Technology may also be influenced by the organization's culture or nature.

The service provider also requires information about the technology used in providing the services. This information should effectively and efficiently support the applied technology, in terms of:

- availability
- reliability
- accessibility        *Standard data stuff*
- timeliness
- accuracy
- relevance

Security or compliance goals often specify the requirements for this  *GDIR-UK* information.

The information and technology dimension relates to the SVS, covering the following aspects:                *So DATA as well- CRUD!*

- information and knowledge
- technologies required
- relationships between different components of the SVS

Organizations should consider the information created, managed, and used by services and the technologies that enable and support these services, when managing and improving the SVS at all levels.

## ■ 3.3   PARTNERS AND SUPPLIERS

Service providers cooperate with partners and suppliers in the design, development, deployment, delivery, support and/or continual improvement of services. This cooperation requires contracts and other agreements.

All of these suppliers and partners need to be integrated, to create a well-balanced service for the customer. This can be achieved through service integration and management.

Integrated services can be managed, using the role of a **service integrator** to ensure that service relationships are properly coordinated.

The role of service integrator may be kept within the organization, but it can also be delegated to a trusted partner.

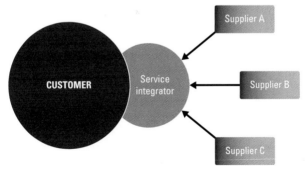

Figure 5.   Service integration and management

In its sourcing strategy, an organization can apply various considerations that are based on its goals, culture and business environment, including:

- **Strategic focus**: be careful not to outsource strategic resources.
- **Corporate culture**: how is working with external parties perceived and how can external parties be part of the organization's culture.
- **Resource scarcity**: sourcing may resolve a shortage of internal resources.
- **Cost concerns**: external resources may be more cost-effective.
- **Subject matter expertise**: activities that are not core may be outsourced; some special expertise may be too expensive to maintain internally.
- **External constraints**: policies may prohibit the outsourcing of specialized activities, e.g. security tasks; alternatively, they may force the organization to use external resources.
- **Demand patterns**: seasonal fluctuations or other constraints may create a case for temporary external resources or service providers.

When relating the partners and suppliers dimension to the SVS, the following aspects should be considered:

- relationships with other organizations
- contracts and agreements
- service integration and management

Partners and suppliers are involved in different phases of services and, therefore, they should be considered when managing and improving the SVS at all levels.

## ■ 3.4   VALUE STREAMS AND PROCESSES

The value streams and processes dimension defines the activities, workflows, controls, and procedures needed to achieve agreed objectives. It is concerned with how the various parts of the organization work in an integrated and coordinated way to enable value creation through products and services.

In practice, the generic service value chain (Figure 9) can follow different patterns, called value streams.

> *Value stream*: A series of steps an organization undertakes to create and deliver products and services to consumers.

Value streams combine the organization's value chain activities. They are specific for given situations and goals, but they may all be examples of the same service value chain.

Value streams should be aimed at maximizing value-adding activities and eliminating waste (non value-adding activities).

Value streams not only apply to the whole service provider organization, they also apply to individual services and products. For each service and product, the following questions should be answered:

- How does the service work: what is its generic delivery?
- Which value streams are involved?
- Who, or what, performs the required service actions?

Value streams can be improved by means of well-defined processes (see Figure 6), which facilitate productivity within and across organizations.

> *Process*: A set of interrelated or interacting activities that transform inputs into outputs.

A process turns defined inputs into defined outputs, and it defines the sequence of actions and their dependencies.

Figure 6. A process

When relating the value streams and processes dimension to the SVS, the following should be considered:
- define activities and workflows
- determine service integration and management
- enable value creation

This dimension is applicable to the SVS in general, as well as to specific products and services, and should be addressed when managing and improving the SVS at all levels.

## ■ 3.5    EXTERNAL FACTORS

The four dimensions of service management are influenced by various external factors. These can be summarized in the PESTLE[4] model:
- **P**olitical factors, e.g. changes in laws and regulations, trade agreements or government provisions.
- **E**conomic factors, e.g. interest rates, international trade agreements or inflation.
- **S**ocial factors, e.g. public opinion, lifestyle or demographic factors.
- **T**echnological factors, e.g. innovations and trends in the use of communication devices.
- **L**egal factors, e.g. new privacy laws.
- **E**nvironmental factors, e.g. energy or waste management issues.

---

4    Also called PESTEL

# 4 The ITIL service value system

Learning outcomes:

- Understand the purpose and components of the ITIL service value system.
- Understand how the ITIL guiding principles can help an organization adopt and adapt service management.
- Understand the activities of the service value chain, and how they interconnect.

Assessment criteria:

- ✔ Describe the ITIL service value system.
- ✔ Describe the nature, use and interaction of the ITIL guiding principles.
- ✔ Explain the use of the seven individual guiding principles.
- ✔ Describe the interconnected nature of the service value chain and how this supports value streams. *PIE - DoD*
- Describe the purpose of each value chain activity.
- Understand the role of continual improvement, and explain the continual improvement model in detail, except how it fits within the service value chain.

## ■ 4.1 SERVICE VALUE SYSTEM OVERVIEW

The ITIL service value system (SVS) describes the systematic approach to value creation, based on the cooperation of all components and activities of the organization. All activities, practices, teams, authorities and responsibilities need to be integrated and coordinated in a systematic approach, to provide the maximum contribution to value.

The key inputs of the SVS are opportunity and demand. The outcome of the
SVS is value. The components of the SVS include:

- the ITIL service value chain
- the ITIL practices
- the ITIL guiding principles
- governance
- continual improvement

The SVS continually improves its service value chain, based on established
practices, governed with a set of guiding principles. It discourages siloed
working and stimulates flexibility. The practices in the SVS can be used all
over the system.

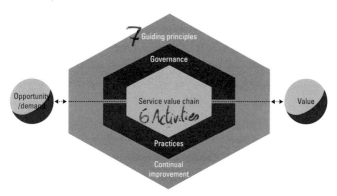

Figure 7. The ITIL service value system (SVS)

## ■ 4.2   OPPORTUNITY AND DEMAND

The SVS (Figure 7) transfers desires and demand into value that is
continually co-created with all stakeholders, through the use and
management of products and services.

**Demand** is the input to the SVS based on opportunities and needs from internal and external stakeholders for products and services.

**Opportunities** represent options or possibilities to add value for stakeholders or otherwise improve the organization.

## ■ 4.3   THE ITIL GUIDING PRINCIPLES

Guiding principles are *recommendations* – not mandates - that can guide an organization in all circumstances, regardless of changes in its goals, strategies, type of work, or management structure.

They are universal, applying to all situations and management levels in an organization, integrating multiple methods into a single service management approach. These principles can be adopted and adapted to a specific organization for their continual improvement initiatives. Organizations should not use just one or two of the seven principles, they should consider the relevance of each of them and how they apply together. Not all principles will be critical in every situation, but they should all be reviewed on each occasion to determine how appropriate they are.

There are seven guiding principles that are part of the SVS:
1. **Focus on value**
   - All activities of the organization should relate to creating value, directly or indirectly, for the organization, its customers and its other stakeholders.
   - All staff should focus on value during operational activities as well as during improvement activities.
   - This requires a solid understanding of the service consumer and the way this consumer uses the service and perceives value, in order to be able to map the organization's efforts in a flexible way to that value specification.
   - The CX and UX both play a role in understanding the value for the consumer.

Customer + User Experience.

2. **Start where you are**
   - The organization should investigate, measure and understand what it already has in place, before starting improvement activities.
   - The current state should, therefore, be measured as objectively as possible, to determine what could be re-used and what should be newly developed.

3. **Progress iteratively with feedback**
   - Improvement should follow an Agile approach, time-boxing small steps in an iterative way, for faster response to stakeholder needs.
   - Feedback loops make part of the output available as input for new improvements, stimulating the insight of staff in their contribution to value creation.
   - Smaller steps stimulate earlier detection of failure, and an overall improvement in quality.
   - The outcome of each iteration must be a *minimum viable product* (MVP): a product with just enough features to satisfy early customers, and to provide feedback for future product development.

4. **Collaborate and promote visibility**
   - Long-term success is stimulated by collaboration between all stakeholders.
   - Each stakeholder's contribution to value creation should be clearly visible, so stakeholders understand the roles of other stakeholders.
   - Workflows and work progress, including backlogs, should be made transparent to relevant stakeholders (e.g. using Kanban boards).
   - Collaboration is more effective if communication, especially on decisions, is visible for all relevant stakeholders.
   - Building trust and removing silos is essential for building collaboration between all stakeholders.

5. **Think and work holistically**
   - A holistic approach requires an understanding of the role of all four dimensions of service management in the SVS, working together in an integrated way.
   - Working holistically requires collaboration between stakeholders.

6.  **Keep it simple and practical**
    -   The number of steps required to deliver outcome-relevant objectives should be kept to a minimum.
    -   Solutions should be kept simple and practical at the beginning, only adding complexity when there are good reasons for it. Avoid focusing on exceptions.
    -   If a component does not provide value or contribute to a useful outcome, eliminate it.
    -   Simplicity stimulates the ease of adoption and can provide quick wins.
    -   Apply this principle to processes, services, actions, activities and metrics.

7.  **Optimize and automate**
    -   Things should only be made as effective and as efficient as makes sense.
    -   Automate frequent and repetitive tasks, to stimulate effectiveness and efficiency, but only after these have been optimized.
    -   Standardization enables automation.
    -   Apply all previous principles, when determining optimal solutions.

*[handwritten margin note: Does it add value to do so?]*

Agile ways of working focus on delivering small, incremental improvements, delivered by small teams. It is a timeboxed, flexible, and adaptive approach that supports rapid change of IT services. Agile ways of working give development teams autonomy and allow them to self-organize. To be effective, Agile teams can apply ITIL principles and practices, just like other teams.

DevOps is an approach to organizing teams that deliver software to live environments, in a close relationship with representatives from the business, development and operations. It applies Agile ways of working with a focus on communication with all involved stakeholders.

ITIL, DevOps and Agile can be great allies. The ITIL guiding principles and the Agile principles can be combined in an effective and modern approach to delivering flexible IT products and services in a close relationship with involved stakeholders.

## ■ 4.4   GOVERNANCE

Organizational governance evaluates, directs, and monitors all the organization's activities, including those of service management (Figure 8).

The ITIL 4 guiding principles and continual improvement can be adopted as a means to determine the organization's own governance principles. The governing body[5] should make sure that the service value chain and the practices are aligned with governance directions, and that the governance body oversees the entire SVS in its continual improvement initiatives.

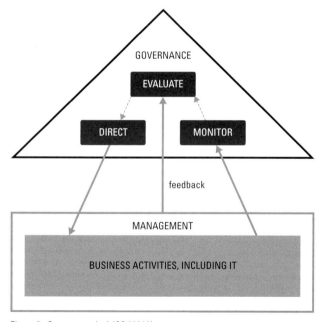

Figure 8.  Governance (ref. ISO 38500)

---

5   Governance differs from management. A governance body may be a Board of Commissioners, a Supervisory Board, an Audit Committee.

## ■ 4.5  SERVICE VALUE CHAIN

The service value chain is the central part of the SVS (Figure 7). It is an operating model that outlines the key activities for managing products and services. It responds to opportunities and demand, and contributes to the value creation. The details of the service value chain are shown in Figure 9.

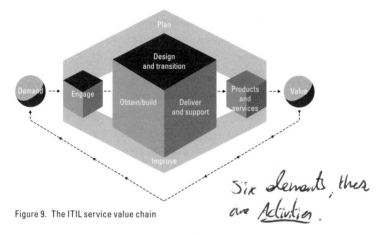

Figure 9. The ITIL service value chain

*Six elements, ther are Activities.*

The ITIL service value chain covers six activities, representing the steps an organization takes in the creation of value:

1. **Plan** - at any level of the service value chain and for all four dimensions and all products and services across the organization.
2. **Improve** - at any level of the service value chain and for all four dimensions and all products and services across the organization.
3. **Engage** - with all involved stakeholders (consumers as well as other stakeholders).
4. **Design and transition** – of products and services, ensuring that these continually meet stakeholder expectations.
5. **Obtain/build** – ensuring that service components are available when and where they are needed, and meet agreed specifications.
6. **Deliver and support** - of services, according to agreed specifications and stakeholders' expectations.

*Demand* **triggers** the delivery of products and services, and – in turn – value. *Products and services*, and - in turn – *value*, are **outputs** of the service value chain. They are not part of the service value chain. The relationship between value and demand also illustrates a feedback loop.

The service value chain activities use combinations of ITIL **practices** to convert their inputs to outputs, contributing to the value creation. They may draw upon internal or external resources, processes, skills or competencies from any combination of practices. E.g., *Engage* may draw upon supplier management, service desk, relationship management, and service request management to respond to *Opportunity and demand*.

ITIL practices are not restricted to any specific activities of the service value chain, they can be used by any of the activities, at any time.

### 4.5.1 Plan

The *Plan* value chain activity applies to all levels of the service value chain of the organization. Its purpose is to ensure a shared understanding of the vision, status, and improvement direction in all four dimensions (Figure 4) and all products and services, in order to co-create value.

*[handwritten: Applies to People + Partners/Supplier]*

Key **inputs** to *Plan* are:

- value chain performance information, improvement initiatives and status reports, and plans, provided by *Improve*
- policies, requirements, and constraints from the governing body
- consolidated demands and opportunities, and knowledge and information about third-party service components, provided by *Engage*
- knowledge and information about new and changed products and services from *Design and transition*, and *Obtain/build*

*[handwritten: Plan + Improve bracket the Engage → Design Transition → Build/Obtain → Run + Maintain it.]*

Key **outputs** of *Plan* arc:

- improvement opportunities for *Improve*
- strategic, tactical, and operational plans, for *all service value chain activities*
- contract and agreement requirements, and a product and service portfolio, for *Engage*
- architectures, policies and portfolio decisions for *Design and transition*

### 4.5.2  Improve

The *Improve* value chain activity also applies to all levels of the service value chain of the organization. Its purpose is to ensure continual improvement of products, services, and practices across all value chain activities and the four dimensions of service management.

The *Improve* value chain activity uses **input** from all value chain activities and other components:

- architectures, policies, portfolio decisions, and strategic, tactical, and operational plans, provided by *Plan*
- knowledge and information about third-party service components, and stakeholders' feedback, provided by *Engage*
- knowledge and information about new and changed products and services from *Design and transition*, and from *Obtain/build*
- product and service performance information, provided by *Deliver and support*
- performance information and improvement opportunities, provided by *all service value chain activities*

Key **outputs** of *Improve* are:

- value chain performance information for *Plan* and for the governing body
- improvement initiatives, plans and improvement status reports, for *all service value chain activities*

- contract and agreement requirements, for *Engage*
- service performance information for *Design and transition*

ITIL 4 supports continual improvement with the ITIL continual improvement model (Figure 10).

### 4.5.3 Engage

The *Engage* value chain activity is the interface with all stakeholders in the service value chain. Its purpose is to provide a good understanding of their needs, transparency, and to continually engage with all stakeholders for effective relationships.

*What do they want ?*

Key **inputs** to *Engage* are:
- interactions with internal and external *customers*:
  - high-level *demand* for services and products
  - detailed *requirements* for services and products
  - marketing opportunities
  - requests and feedback
- interactions with *users*:
  - incidents, service requests, and feedback
- interactions with *partners* and *suppliers*:
  - cooperation opportunities and feedback
  - knowledge and information about third party service components
- architectures, policies, portfolio decisions, and strategic, tactical, and operational plans, provided by *Plan*
- improvements initiatives, plans and status reports, from *Improve*
- knowledge and information about new and changed products and services, from *Design and transition* and straight from *Obtain/build*
- product and service performance information, and information on the completion of user support tasks, from *Deliver and support*
- contract and agreement requirements, from *all service value chain activities*

Key **outputs** of *Engage* are:

- service performance reports, for *customers*
- consolidated demands and opportunities, for *Plan*
- improvement opportunities and stakeholders' feedback, for *Improve*
- change or project initiation requests, for *Obtain/build*
- product and service requirements, for *Design and transition*
- user support tasks, for *Deliver and support*
- contracts and agreements with all suppliers and partners, and knowledge and information about third-party service components, for *all service value chain activities*

### 4.5.4  Design and transition

The *Design and transition* value chain activity is concerned with designing and redesigning products and services, so they can be used in a production environment. Its purpose is to ensure that products and services continually meet stakeholder expectations for quality, costs, and time to market. *By designing them to do so*

Key **inputs** to *Design and transition* are:

- architectures, policies, portfolio decisions, and strategic, tactical, and operational plans, provided by *Plan*
- improvement initiatives, plans, and status reports, provided by *Improve*
- product and service requirements, contracts and agreements with external and internal suppliers and partners, and knowledge and information about third-party service components, provided by *Engage*
- service components, and knowledge and information about new and changed products and services, from *Obtain/build*
- service performance information, provided by *Deliver and support*

Key **outputs** of *Design and transition* are:

- performance information and improvement opportunities, for *Improve*
- contract and agreement requirements, for *Engage*
- requirements and specifications, for *Obtain/build*
- new and changed products and services, for *Deliver and support*

- knowledge and information about new and changed products and services, *to all service value chain activities*

### 4.5.5 Obtain/build

The *Obtain/build* value chain activity produces and or acquires the components for the products and services. Its purpose is to ensure that these components are available when and where they are needed, and meet agreed specifications.

*So get what you have designed!*

Key **inputs** to *Obtain/build* are:
- goods and services provided by external and internal *suppliers* and *partners*
- architectures, policies, portfolio decisions, and strategic, tactical, and operational plans, provided by *Plan*
- improvement initiatives and plans, and status reports, provided by *Improve*
- contracts and agreements with external and internal suppliers and partners, change or project initiation requests, and knowledge and information about third-party service components, provided by *Engage*
- requirements and specifications, and knowledge and information about new and changed products and services, provided by *Design and transition*
- change requests, provided by *Deliver and support*

Key **outputs** of *Obtain/build* are:
- performance information and improvement opportunities, for *Improve*
- contract and agreement requirements, for *Engage*
- service components, for *Design and transition* or straight to *Deliver and support*
- knowledge and information about new and changed service components, to *all service value chain activities*

### 4.5.6 Deliver and support

The *Deliver and support* value chain activity handles the operational environment, where the products and services are made available for the customers. Its purpose is to ensure that services are delivered and supported according to agreed specifications and stakeholders' expectations.

Key **inputs** to *Deliver and support* are:

- improvement initiatives and status reports, provided by *Improve*
- knowledge and information about third-party service components, and user support tasks, provided by *Engage*
- service components, provided by *Obtain/build*
- new and changed products and services provided by *Design and transition*
- knowledge and information about new and changed service components and services, from *Obtain/build* or from *Design and transition*

Key **outputs** of *Deliver and support* are:
- services delivered to *customers* and *users*
- improvement opportunities, for *Improve*
- product and service performance information, for *Improve* and *Engage* and for *Design and transition*
- contract and agreement requirements, and information on the completion of user support tasks, for *Engage*
- change requests, for *Obtain/build* or *Design and transition*

## ■ 4.6 VALUE STREAMS AND THE SERVICE VALUE CHAIN

In the service value chain, many different value streams can be created as a series of steps that an organization takes in the creation of value. Each step transforms inputs into outputs. A value stream can be composed by any set of service value chain activities, in any sequence, in any iteration of activities.

*Engage* may trigger *Delivery and support* (e.g. for support tasks) and then revert to *Engage* for follow-up (e.g. with information on the completion of user support tasks). *Engage* may also trigger *Obtain/build* (e.g. for change or project initiation), subsequently follow this by *Delivery and support* (e.g. handling service components), and then revert to additional *Obtain/build* (e.g. with additional change request).

This way, a wide variety of value streams may be created to adjust the products and services and their support to the demands of the customer, co-creating value. Each of these value streams can be supported by ITIL practices, for a specific scenario. Inputs and outputs can be specific for such a scenario.

## ■ 4.7   CONTINUAL IMPROVEMENT

Continual improvement takes place all over the organization and the SVS. It applies to all components of the service value chain and to all relationships with stakeholders. It can be triggered at any time by any individual or stakeholder party.

Continual improvement is supported by:

1.  the ITIL continual improvement model (shown in Figure 10), providing organizations with a structured approach to implementing improvements
2.  the *Improve* value chain activity (see sub-section 4.5.2), embedding continual improvement into the value chain
3.  the continual improvement practice (see sub-section 5.1.2), supporting organizations in their day-to-day improvement efforts

The generic goal: support continual improvement at all levels.

The ITIL continual improvement model supports an iterative approach, focusing upon customer value. It is linked to the organization's vision. The model is not prescriptive in a linear sense: steps can be taken repeatedly until they provide the desired result. Logic and common sense should always prevail when using the continual improvement model.

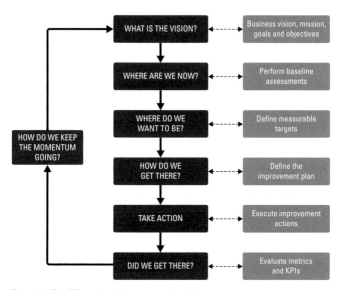

Figure 10. The ITIL continual improvement model

## ■ 4.8  PRACTICES

Practices are sets of organizational resources designed for performing work or accomplishing an objective. They can be used to support the activities in the service value chain. Chapter 5 describes how 34 ITIL practices are grouped into the following three categories:

- 14 general management practices
- 17 service management practices
- 3 technical management practices

# 5    ITIL management practices

Learning outcomes:
- Know the purpose and key terms of 15 ITIL practices
- Understand seven ITIL practices

Assessment criteria:
- Recall the **purpose** of the following ITIL practices: Information security management, Relationship management, Supplier management, Monitoring and event management, Release management, Service configuration management, Deployment management, Continual improvement, Change control, Incident management, Problem management, Service request management, Service desk, Service level management
- Recall **definitions** of the following ITIL terms: IT asset, Event, Configuration item (CI), Change, Incident, Problem, Known error
- Explain the following ITIL practices **in detail**, excluding how they fit within the service value chain: Continual improvement including the continual improvement model, Change control, Incident management, Problem management, Service request management, Service desk, Service level management

ITIL 4 defines a set of 34 practices that can be used to support all activities of the service value chain, as required by service value streams.

An **ITIL practice** is a set of organizational resources designed for performing work or accomplishing an objective.

The resources of a practice are based on the four dimensions of service management (Figure 4). A practice can contribute to any value chain activity, it is not uniquely linked to any of them.

These 34 practices are broken up into three categories.

There are 14 **general management practices**:
1. architecture management
2. continual improvement *(+ model)*
3. information security management
4. knowledge management
5. measurement and reporting
6. organizational change management
7. portfolio management
8. project management
9. relationship management
10. risk management
11. service financial management
12. strategy management
13. supplier management
14. workforce and talent management

*Apply anywhere*

There are 17 **service management practices** that are specific for the service management domain:
1. availability management
2. business analysis
3. capacity and performance management
4. change control
5. incident management
6. IT asset management

*To a service*

7. monitoring and event management
8. problem management
9. release management
10. service catalogue management
11. service configuration management
12. service continuity management
13. service design
14. service desk
15. service level management
16. service request management
17. service validation and testing

*= Need to know the Detail.

*= Need to know the purpose

⊘ = know Definition See glossary.

There are 3 **technical management practices** that have been elevated from a technology focused function to a wider applicable practice:

1. deployment management
2. infrastructure and platform management
3. software development and management

Techie !

The categories are used to group the practices together, according to their origination. However the practices themselves should be used in any combination that suits the service management strategy of the organization.

They are presented in alphabetical order, again emphasizing that there is no logical sequence in applying the practices; they can be used in any order and in any combination.

## ■ 5.1   GENERAL MANAGEMENT PRACTICES

General management practices have been adopted from the general business management domain to be applied in the service management domain.

The ITIL 4 Foundation exam requires that candidates can recall the **purpose** of the following four general management practices (*presented in alphabetical order*):

- continual improvement
- information security management
- relationship management
- supplier management

The remaining 10 general management practices are not examined.

Candidates should also be able to explain *one* general management practice **in detail,** excluding how it fits within the service value chain, this being:

- continual improvement, including the continual improvement model (Figure 10)

### 5.1.1  Architecture management

The **purpose** of the architecture management practice is to provide an understanding of all the different elements that make up an organization and how those elements interrelate, enabling the organization to effectively achieve its current and future objectives.

It provides the principles, standards, and tools that enable an organization to manage complex change in a structured and Agile way.

A complete architecture management practice should address all architecture domains:

- business architecture
- service architecture
- information systems architecture, including data and applications architectures
- technology architecture
- environmental architecture

This practice has a high interaction with service value chain activities *Plan*, *Improve*, *Design and transition*, and a medium interaction with *Engage*, *Obtain/build* and *Deliver and support*.

## 5.1.2 Continual improvement

*All* [handwritten]

> The **purpose** of the continual improvement practice is to align the organization's practices and services with changing business needs through the ongoing identification and improvement of services, service components, practices, or any element involved in the efficient and effective management of products and services.

Organizations that adopt a culture of continual improvement will not only focus on opportunities, they will also need to establish practices that go with it. This means that the organization needs to:

- make all staff aware of the value of continual improvement
- invest in continual improvement, in terms of time and money
- manage improvement activities in a structured way

The handling of logged improvement opportunities should be structured and coordinated across the organization, based upon the approaches commonly taken to risk management:

1. identify and log opportunities
2. assess and prioritize
3. set up business cases for improvement options
4. plan and implement selected initiatives
5. measure and evaluate results

*Same as for Risks/opportunities* [handwritten]

This approach should be adopted at all levels of the organization: continual improvement is the responsibility of all staff, and it should be reflected throughout their attitude, behavior and culture. We have already described the role of the continual improvement model in section 4.7.

Continual improvement should be reflected in all instruments, techniques, methods and models the organization applies. This includes:

- Lean methods, reducing waste
- multi-phase projects with iterative, Agile techniques
- assessment and evaluation techniques for determining the stages of development and maturity, including balanced scorecard, SWOT analysis and quick wins
- DevOps approaches to organization structures

*All underlie iterative principle*

The organization's management should support continual improvement initiatives by:

- leading the way, making continual improvement the normal approach to all work
- assigning coordination responsibilities, making a dedicated team responsible for managing and coordinating improvement initiatives
- offering training to their staff, and making continual improvement part of everyone's job
- involving internal as well as external stakeholders in a structured way, embedding continual improvement in formalized relationships (contracts)

Improvement ideas can be registered in a **continual improvement register** (CIR): this is a database or structured document used to log, track and manage improvement ideas from identification through to final action, demonstrating their status and progress. As with the configuration management system (CMS, see sub-section 5.2.11), this CIR can be composed of various registrations that are maintained at various levels of the organization.

Registration and management should follow regular techniques that are used in many other practices, including prioritization techniques based on impact and urgency.

The continual improvement practice is related to various other practices, including problem management (for identification of improvement opportunities), change control and organizational change management (for implementing improvements), and project management (for organizing and managing the improvements).

Continual improvement interacts highly with *all service value chain activities.*

### 5.1.3 Information security management

The **purpose** of the information security management practice is to protect the information required by the organization to conduct its business.

The information security management practice focuses on handling the risks to core aspects of information security, including:

- confidentiality
- integrity
- availability
- authentication
- non-repudiation

Information security management should be balanced between **prevention**, **detection**, and **correction**, using restrictions but still allowing for innovation, and aligned to the organization's risk appetite.

Information security management interacts with all other practices, and is critically dependent on the behavior of people throughout the organization.

Just as with the continual improvement practice, information security management interacts highly with *all service value chain activities.*

### 5.1.4    Knowledge management

The **purpose** of the knowledge management practice is to maintain and improve the effective, efficient, and convenient use of information and knowledge across the organization.

Knowledge management supports a structured approach to defining, building, re-using, and sharing knowledge in various forms. Knowledge is more than just storing information or data. It is all about making sure that the required information, skills, practices and solutions are used *in their context*. Knowledge is one of the most valuable assets of an organization.

The practice has a high interaction with service value chain activities *Improve* and *Deliver and support*, and a medium interaction with *Plan*, *Engage*, *Obtain/build*, and *Design and transition*.

### 5.1.5    Measurement and reporting

The **purpose** of the measurement and reporting practice is to support effective decision-making and continual improvement by decreasing the levels of uncertainty.

This is achieved through the collection of relevant metrics on various managed objects and the valid assessment of this data in an appropriate context. Managed objects include, but are not limited to, products and services, practices and service value chain activities, teams and individuals, suppliers and partners, and the organization as a whole.

Measurement techniques include the definition of critical success factors (CSFs) and the related key performance indicators (KPIs).

> *Critical success factor* (CSF): *A necessary precondition for the achievement of intended results.*
>
> *Key performance indicator* (KPI): *An important metric used to evaluate the success in meeting an objective.*

Reports and dashboards should be restricted to relevant content, supporting effective decision-making.

The practice has a high interaction with service value chain activities *Plan, Improve, Obtain/build* and *Design and transition*, and a medium interaction with *Engage* and *Deliver and support*.

### 5.1.6 Organizational change management

The **purpose** of the organizational change management practice is to ensure that changes in an organization are smoothly and successfully implemented, and that lasting benefits are achieved by managing the human aspects of the changes.

Organizational change management focuses on the acceptance and support of changes to organizational aspects by every involved individual. It handles resistance to change by the removal of obstacles and the stimulation of acceptance through training and awareness. To be successful, it requires:

- **clear and relevant objectives**, making sense to all stakeholders and creating a sense of urgency
- **strong and committed leadership**, through the actively demonstrated support of sponsors and leaders
- **willing and prepared participants**, who understand why the change is necessary and how they contribute to it
- **sustained improvement**, preventing fallback scenarios by continual reinforcement of the value of the change

People are essential to the success of changes.

The practice has a high interaction with service value chain activity *Improve,* a medium interaction with the activities *Plan, Engage, Design and transition*, and a low interaction with *Obtain/build* and *Deliver and support.*

### 5.1.7  Portfolio management

> The **purpose** of the portfolio management practice is to ensure that the
> organization has the appropriate mix of programs, projects, products, and services
> to execute the organization's strategy within its funding and resource constraints.

Portfolio management makes sure that all products, services, programs and products are aligned to support strategic goals, and oversees the allocation, deployment and management of resources across the organization. It encompasses several portfolios, including:

- **product/service portfolio**, covering all products and services that are managed by the organization
- **project portfolio**, overseeing all authorized projects and ensuring that these achieve their planned goals.
- **customer portfolio**, with all the organization's internal and external customers, maintained by the relationship management practice.

The practice has a high interaction with service value chain activity *Plan*, a medium interaction with *Improve, Engage, Obtain/build, Design and transition*, and a low interaction with *Deliver and support.*

### 5.1.8  Project management

> The **purpose** of the project management practice is to ensure that all projects in the
> organization are successfully delivered.

This is achieved by planning, delegating, monitoring, and maintaining control of all aspects of a project, and ensuring the people involved are sufficiently motivated.

Projects can be used to manage significant changes to any component. They can be part of a larger program or a project portfolio. Traditional waterfall methods have been extended with Agile methods, specifically when requirements are uncertain in a rapidly changing environment.

The practice has a high interaction with service value chain activities *Obtain/build* and *Design and transition*, and medium interaction with *Plan*, *Improve*, *Engage* and *Deliver and support*.

### 5.1.9   Relationship management

The **purpose** of the relationship management practice is to establish and nurture the links between the organization and its stakeholders at both strategic and tactical levels.

It includes the identification, analysis, monitoring, and continual improvement of relationships with and between stakeholders.

Relationship management applies to all stakeholders, internal and external. It focuses on handling all needs, priorities, complaints and escalations in the context of service value creation, in such a way that all stakeholders are satisfied.

The *business relationship manager* (BRM) is a common role, responsible for maintaining good relationships with one or more customers.

The practice contributes to all service value chain activities and multiple value streams. It has a high impact on *Plan*, *Improve*, *Engage*, and *Design and transition*, and medium interaction with *Obtain/build* and *Deliver and support*.

### 5.1.10 Risk management

> The **purpose** of the risk management practice is to ensure that the organization understands and effectively handles risks.

Risk is not only associated with **threats**, but also with **opportunities**. Risks need to be identified, assessed and treated, in such a way that the benefits outweigh the costs of the risks.

ISO 31000:2018 provides guidelines for risk management.

Risk management is an integral part of all organizational activities and, therefore, central to the organization's SVS.

The practice has a high interaction with *all* service value chain activities.

### 5.1.11 Service financial management

> The **purpose** of the service financial management practice is to support the organization's strategies and plans for service management by ensuring that the organization's financial resources and investments are being used effectively.

Service financial management is responsible for managing the budgeting, costing, accounting, and charging activities of an organization, and is a common language used to communicate with stakeholders.

The practice has a high interaction with the service value chain activity *Plan*, and a medium interaction with the other five activities.

### 5.1.12 Strategy management

The **purpose** of the strategy management practice is to formulate the goals of the organization and adopt the courses of action and allocation of resources necessary for achieving those goals.

Strategy management establishes the organization's direction, identifies opportunities and constraints, translates strategic plans into tactical and operational plans, defines or clarifies the organization's priorities, and provides consistency or guidance in an Agile response to the changing environment.

The practice has a high interaction with the service value chain activity *Plan*, and a medium interaction with all other service value chain activities.

### 5.1.13 Supplier management

The **purpose** of the supplier management practice is to ensure that the organization's suppliers and their performances are managed appropriately to support the seamless provision of quality products and services.

This includes creating closer, more collaborative relationships with key suppliers to uncover and realize new value and reduce the risk of failure, supported by:

- **communication**, through creating a single point of visibility and control
- a **supplier strategy** (sourcing strategy) with policies and management information
- **agreements** with internal and external suppliers
- managing **supplier performance**

*So not in strategy Management.*

A sourcing strategy may include various supplier relationships, including:

- insourcing
- outsourcing

- single source or partnership
- multi-sourcing

Suppliers should be evaluated and selected, based on importance and impact of the supplier's services, and the associated risks and costs.

Section 3.3 and Figure 5 describe the role of the **service integrator**, who is responsible for coordinating and orchestrating all suppliers involved in the organization's service management.

Of the four dimensions of service management (Figure 4), supplier management particularly affects the partners and suppliers dimension.

The practice has a high interaction with service value chain activities *Plan*, *Engage*, *Obtain/build*, *Design and transition*, *Deliver and support*, and a medium interaction with *Improve*.

### 5.1.14 Workforce and talent management

The **purpose** of the workforce and talent management practice is to ensure that the organization has the right people with the appropriate skills and knowledge and in the correct roles to support its business objectives.

The practice focuses on managing employees and people resources, including planning, recruitment, onboarding, learning and development, performance measurement, and succession planning. Having the right talent available at the right time in the right place is becoming critical in supporting the digitization of organizations in modern economies.

---

***Organizational velocity:*** *The speed, effectiveness, and efficiency with which an organization operates.*

---

Organizational velocity influences time to market, quality, safety, costs, and risks. The leaders and managers at every level throughout the organization should be responsible for the management of workforce and talent, and their competencies, skills, abilities, knowledge and attitude.

---

**Competencies**: The combination of observable and measurable knowledge, skills, abilities, and attitudes that contribute to enhanced employee performance and ultimately result in organizational success.

**Skills**: A developed proficiency or dexterity in thought, verbal communication, or physical action.

**Ability**: The power or aptitude to perform physical or mental activities related to a profession or trade.

**Knowledge**: The understanding of facts or information acquired by a person through experience or education; the theoretical or practical understanding of a subject.

**Attitude**: A set of emotions, beliefs, and behaviors towards a particular object, person, thing, or event.

---

The practice has a high interaction with service value chain activities *Plan* and *Improve*, and a medium interaction with the other activities.

## ■ 5.2   SERVICE MANAGEMENT PRACTICES

ITIL 4 describes 17 service management practices that are specific for the service management domain.

The ITIL 4 Foundation exam requires that candidates can recall the **purpose** of the following nine practices (*presented in alphabetical order*):

- change control
- incident management

- IT asset management
- monitoring and event management
- problem management
- release management
- service desk
- service level management
- service request management

The remaining eight service management practices are not examined.

Of these nine practices, candidates should be able to explain the following six practices **in detail**, excluding how they fit within the service value chain:
- change control
- incident management
- problem management
- service desk
- service level management
- service request management

Of the remaining three practices (IT asset management, monitoring and event management, and release management), only the purpose statements are examined.

Candidates should also be able to recall the **definitions** of the following ITIL terms:
- IT asset
- event
- configuration item
- change
- incident
- problem
- known error

### 5.2.1 Availability management

> The **purpose** of the availability management practice is to ensure that services
> deliver agreed levels of availability to meet the needs of customers and users.

Availability relates directly to the service being there as agreed or not, and
it can be measured by means of two metrics: mean time between failures
(MTBF) and mean time to restore service (MTRS).

> *Availability*: The ability of an IT service or other configuration item to perform its
> agreed function when required.

Availability incorporates a wide range of activities, from negotiating
availability in agreements and designing the required infrastructure, up to
monitoring, analyzing, reporting and improving the agreed availability.

Availability management can be integrated with other practices like risk
management, service continuity management, or capacity and performance
management. It also relates closely with incident and problem management.

The practice has a high interaction with service value chain activity *Plan*, a
medium interaction with *Improve*, *Obtain/build*, *Design and transition* and
*Deliver and support*, and a low interaction with *Engage*.

### 5.2.2 Business analysis

> The **purpose** of the business analysis practice is to analyze a business or some
> element of it, define its associated needs, and recommend solutions to address
> these needs and/or solve a business problem, which must facilitate value creation
> for stakeholders.

Business analysis key activities include the analysis of the customer's
business and the performance of current products and services, and

identifying and prioritizing improvements that can be made with products and services.

Business requirements can be utility-focused or warranty-focused.

> **Warranty requirements**: Typically non-functional requirements captured as inputs from key stakeholders and other practices.
>
> **Utility requirements**: Functional requirements which have been defined by the customer and are unique to a specific product.

The practice has a high interaction with service value chain activities *Plan*, *Engage*, *Obtain/build*, *Design and transition*, and a medium interaction with *Improve* and *Deliver and support*.

### 5.2.3  Capacity and performance management

The **purpose** of the capacity and performance management practice is to ensure that services achieve agreed and expected performance levels, satisfying current and future demand in a cost-effective way.

Service performance depends on service capacity, which is defined as the maximum throughput that a CI or service can deliver.

> **Performance**: A measure of what is achieved or delivered by a system, person, team, practice, or service.

Service performance relates to the quantified volume of service actions in a given timeframe, and the time required to fulfill certain service actions. It usually deals with the performance of not only the service, but also the underpinning infrastructure, provided internally or externally.

Capacity and performance management activities include the analysis of current service and infrastructure performance and the planning of improvements. It is usually highly integrated with continual improvement, risk management, change control, problem management and service continuity management practices.

The practice has a high interaction with service value chain activity *Improve*, and a medium interaction with the other five activities.

### 5.2.4  Change control

> The **purpose** of the change control practice is to maximize the number of successful service and product changes by ensuring that risks have been properly assessed, authorizing changes to proceed, and managing the change schedule.

The scope of change control is defined by each organization, but it usually focuses on products and services. It will typically include all IT infrastructure, applications, documentation, processes, supplier relationships, and anything else that might directly or indirectly impact a product or service.

Change control differs from the organizational change management practice that manages the people aspects of changes, to ensure that improvements and organizational transformation initiatives are implemented successfully.

> **Change**: The addition, modification, or removal of anything that could have a direct or indirect effect on services.

Change control balances the need to make changes with the requirement to protect customers and users from the adverse effect of these changes. It assesses the involved risks and expected benefits, and it requires authorization by a **change authority**, before deploying a changed component. A change authority is a person or group responsible for authorizing a change.

Three types of change can be distinguished, and each of them may have a different change authority assigned:

- **Standard changes**: low-risk, pre-authorized changes that are well understood and fully documented, and can be implemented without needing additional authorization or risk assessment. They may be initiated as service requests.
- **Normal changes**: changes following the standard process of scheduling, assessing, and authorization, initiated by a change request. *Change models*, covering predefined roles for assessment and authorization, may be set up for specific changes, depending upon the risks involved.
- **Emergency changes**: changes that must be implemented as soon as possible, for various possible reasons. Emergency changes are handled at high speed but, as far as possible, they are subject to the same testing, assessment, and authorization as normal changes. Less impactful activities may be delayed.

A **change model** is a repeatable approach to the management of a particular type of change. *How to run a change*

Changes are planned in a **change schedule**, to support communication, avoid conflicts, assign resources, and to provide information needed for other practices. A change schedule is a calendar that shows planned and historical changes.

A change is described and requested using a **request for change** (RFC).

Organizations that have an automated pipeline for **continuous integration and continuous deployment** often automate most steps of the change control process.

The practice has a high interaction with service value chain activities *Improve, Obtain/build, Design and transition, Deliver and support*, and a low interaction with *Plan* and *Engage*.

## 5.2.5 Incident management *All*

> The **purpose** of incident management is to minimize the negative impact of incidents by restoring normal service operation as quickly as possible.

Incidents can significantly impact the value that should be created in the SVS. As a consequence, they should be managed carefully.

> *Incident*: An unplanned interruption to a service or reduction in the quality of a service.

Incidents should be logged, prioritized and managed, so they can be resolved according to customer and user expectations. These expectations should be agreed and managed carefully in terms of *target resolution times* that reflect business impact.

Incidents may be categorized by their impact and their corresponding priority (e.g. 1, 2, 3), and by their nature, (e.g. information security incidents). *Low impact* incidents should be managed as efficiently as possible, so resources can be made available for the management of incidents with *larger impact*. *Major incidents* as well as security incidents may be supported by dedicated processes.

Incident information should be registered in incident records, in the database of a suitable tool. To facilitate quick resolution of the incident, this tool should preferably support matching between incident records and enable links to related CIs and to records of other practices, including changes, problems, and known errors.

The stored information is important for the matching of future incidents, and for other practices, including problem management, knowledge management, risk management, availability management, service continuity management and continual improvement.

Incident resolution can involve resources from all over the organization and its environment. This may include *self-help* by users, support by a service desk agent, by a *support team* with more expertise or authorization, or by other stakeholders like suppliers. Other techniques such as swarming, involving resources from various teams and stakeholders, may also be applied.

An incident with extremely high impact may evoke a *disaster recovery plan*, which is prepared by the service continuity practice.

Dealing with incidents is possible in every service value chain activity, but the most visible incidents are those that happen in an operational environment, with a direct effect on users.

The practice has a high interaction with service value chain activities *Engage* and *Deliver and support*, and medium interaction with *Improve*, *Obtain*/build and *Design and transition*. There is no significant interaction with the service value chain activity *Plan*.

### 5.2.6 IT asset management

The **purpose** of the IT asset management practice is to plan and manage the full lifecycle of all IT assets, in order to help the organization:

- maximize value
- control costs
- manage risks

- support decision-making regarding the purchase, re-use, and retirement of assets
- meet regulatory and contractual requirements

The scope of IT asset management (ITAM) typically includes all hardware, software (software asset management, SAM), licenses, networks, cloud services, and client devices, but it may also include non-IT assets such as buildings or information where these have a financial value and are required to deliver an IT service, or devices that are part of the Internet of Things (IoT). In all cases, the full lifecycle of each asset should be managed.

> **IT asset**: Any financially valuable component that can contribute to the delivery of an IT product or service.

Reliable information on assets should be kept available in an **IT asset register**, which is often combined with a configuration management system (CMS) This requires a good interface with other practices, including service configuration management, incident management, change control, and deployment management, as well as a regular audit of the register's content.

The practice has a high interaction with service value chain activities *Obtain/build* and *Design and transition*, a medium interaction with *Plan* and *Deliver and support*, and a low interaction with *Improve* and *Engage*.

### 5.2.7 Monitoring and event management  *of Service*

The **purpose** of the monitoring and event management practice is to systematically observe services and service components, and record and report selected changes of state that are identified as events.

Event = change from steady state.

This practice identifies and prioritizes infrastructure, service, business process, and information security events, and establishes the appropriate response to those events, including responding to conditions that could lead to potential faults or incidents.

> **Event**: *Any change of state that has significance for the management of a service or other configuration item (CI).*

Events are typically recognized through notifications created by an IT service, CI, or monitoring tool.

Events can be categorized after the impact of the observation:

- **informational events**, without the need for an action
- **warning events**, indicating that a consequence can be prevented if action is taken
- **exception events**, indicating a negative effect (an incident) that requires immediate action (e.g. initiate the incident management practice)

Monitoring focuses on the systematic observation of services and related CIs, to detect conditions of potential significance. Monitoring can be done actively or passively. It can be automated to a high degree.

Event management focuses on recording and managing events, determining their significance, and identifying and initiating the correct control action to manage them. This includes the initiation of incident management in the case of a serious exception event, triggering problem management with event data, or initiating a change.

The practice has a high interaction with the service value chain activity *Deliver and support*, a medium interaction with *Improve* and *Design and transition*, and a low interaction with *Engage* and *Obtain/build*. There is no significant interaction with the service value chain activity *Plan*.

### 5.2.8  Problem management  *[handwritten: All]*

*[handwritten note top right: Incidents → Problem → known Error]*

> The **purpose** of problem management is to reduce the likelihood and impact of incidents by identifying actual and potential causes of incidents, and managing workarounds and known errors.

Any of the four service management dimensions (Figure 4) may cause errors (flaws, imperfections) that may introduce threats to value creation. In ITIL, these errors are called problems.

> *Problem*: A cause, or potential cause, of one or more incidents.

*[handwritten note right: So not cause of incidents!]*

Problems have an indirect, future impact on services: they are defined as causes. The *symptoms* of these causes are the incidents that *do* have an impact on service quality.

As soon as a problem is analyzed and the root cause is understood and identified, its status changes to *known error*, and its resolution can be started.

> *Known error*: A problem that has been analyzed but has not been resolved.

Problem management has three phases (Figure 11):
1.  **Problem identification** may involve trend analysis, investigation into recurring or major incidents, or investigating any other (third-party) source of information. This phase delivers identified and logged problems.
2.  **Problem control** prioritizes the handling of logged problems, analyzes them from all four dimensions, and determines the known error.
3.  **Error control** then follows up with the resolution of the known error by identifying potential solutions, selecting measures to reduce the impact of known errors by means of business case analysis, and initiating the implementation of selected measures (e.g. via change control).

*[handwritten note right: POPIT + partner/supplier]*

Figure 11. The phases of problem management

If the solutions are not permanent or have limited effect, the error control phase continues to monitor the known error, re-assessing its effect and improving temporary measures (workarounds).

> **Workaround**: A solution that reduces or eliminates the impact of an incident or problem for which a full resolution is not yet available.

Workarounds relate to the reduction of impact, but they may also contribute to incident prevention, reducing the likelihood of the incident. Workarounds may be defined at any stage (each of the phases of Figure 11), they are logged in the problem record, and they are subject to regular re-assessment. If there is no definitive solution available, workarounds can become the permanent way of dealing with the problem.

Prioritization of problem handling is based on the involved risk, measured as a combination of potential impact and probability.

Problem management interacts with several other practices, including incident management, knowledge management, risk management and change control. Problem management activities may also identify improvement opportunities, which are included in a continual improvement register (CIR).

The practice has a high interaction with service value chain activities *Improve* and *Deliver and support*, a medium interaction with *Engage*, and a low interaction with *Obtain/build* and *Design and transition*. There is no significant interaction with the service value chain activity *Plan*.

## 5.2.9  Release management

The **purpose** of the release management practice is to make new and changed services and features available for use.

A release is planned in a **release plan**, with detailed **release schedules** that are agreed with customers and other stakeholders. Releases may comprise many different components, including infrastructure, software, documentation, training, and tools.

> **Release**: A version of a service or other configuration item, or a collection of configuration items, that is made available for use.

Releases are implemented in the deployment management practice.

In a DevOps environment, release management is often integrated with a continuous integration/continuous delivery approach.

The practice has a high interaction with the service value chain activity *Design and transition,* a medium interaction with *Plan*, *Obtain/build* and *Deliver and support*, and a low interaction with *Improve* and *Engage*.

### 5.2.10  Service catalogue management

The **purpose** of service catalogue management is to provide a single source of consistent information on all services and service offerings, and to ensure that it is available to the relevant audience.

The **service catalogue** provides a view on the scope of what services are available, and on what terms. It may be made available to different stakeholders with different views, including:

- **user views**, to support requests for various service offerings
- **customer views**, with information on service levels and financial data

- **IT to IT customer views,** for detailed technical information, used in service delivery

The user view is often supported by a listing of consumable or orderable elements of service offerings. This is often called the request catalogue.

> *Request catalogue:* A view of the service catalogue, providing details on service requests for existing and new services, which is made available for the user.

The practice has a high interaction with the service value chain activity *Engage,* a medium interaction with *Design and transition* and *Deliver and support,* and a low interaction with *Plan, Improve,* and *Obtain/build.*

### 5.2.11 Service configuration management

The **purpose** of the service configuration management practice is to ensure that accurate and reliable information about the configuration of services, and the CIs that support them, is available when and where it is needed.

Service configuration management makes information available on how configuration items (CIs) are configured and how they are related, to clarify how they contribute to create value.

> *Configuration item* (CI): Any component that needs to be managed, in order to deliver an IT service.

CIs include the services, and the contributing components from any of the four dimensions, covering hardware, software, networks, buildings, people, suppliers, and documentation. The image of how these components contribute to the service is called a service map or service model.

Service configuration management supports many of the other ITIL practices, making essential information on the service components available, and linking CIs to logged incidents, problems, and changes. This information may be stored in the configuration management system (CMS).

> ***Configuration management system*** *(CMS): A set of tools, data, and information that is used to support service configuration management.*

The CMS may include a single **configuration management database** (CMDB) for the whole organization, but it may also include various sources. All information should, preferably, be made available in an integrated way, to authorized staff.

The cost of registration should not outweigh the value that the information in the CMS creates. Information may be stored manually in the CMS, but it can also be collected by tools.

The practice has a high interaction with service value chain activities *Obtain/build* and *Design and transition,* a medium interaction with *Improve* and *Deliver and support*, and a low interaction with *Plan* and *Engage.*

### 5.2.12 Service continuity management

> The **purpose** of the service continuity management practice is to ensure that the availability and performance of a service is maintained at a sufficient level in the event of a disaster.

Service continuity management comes into action when normal response and recovery practices such as incident and major incident management are no longer adequate.

An organizational event of this magnitude is typically referred to as a **disaster**: a sudden unplanned event that causes great damage or serious loss to an organization (definition by the Business Continuity Institute).

Service continuity management supports the overall business continuity management (BCM) by assuring that IT services can be resumed according to business requirements, following a disaster. Organizations should define, agree and document what is considered to be a disaster, as well as the actions that follow should it actually occur, separate from the agreed way of handling (major) incidents.

Key components of service continuity management include:

---

*Recovery time objective* (RTO): The maximum acceptable period of time following a service disruption that can elapse before the lack of business functionality severely impacts the organization.

*Recovery point objective* (RPO) The point to which information used by an activity must be restored to enable the activity to operate on resumption.

*Disaster recovery plans*: A set of clearly defined plans related to how an organization will recover from a disaster as well as return to a pre-disaster condition, considering the four dimensions of service management.

*Business impact analysis* (BIA): The activity that identifies vital business functions (VBFs) and their dependencies, in terms of requirements that include RTOs, RPOs, and minimum target service levels for each IT service.

---

The practice has no high interaction with service value chain activities, medium interactions with *Plan, Improve, Obtain/build, Design and transition* and *Deliver and support*, and a low interaction with *Engage*.

### 5.2.13 Service design

The **purpose** of the service design practice is to design products and services that are fit for purpose, fit for use, and that can be delivered by the organization and its ecosystem.

This includes planning and organizing people, partners and suppliers, information, communication, technology, and practices for new or changed products and services, and the interaction between the organization and its customers.

The service design practice should ensure that the customer's journey is as pleasant and frictionless as it can be. Techniques that can be used for service design include **design thinking** and focusing on **customer experience** (CX) and **user experience** (UX and Lean UX).

Service design should integrate with risk management practices in all its activities.

The practice has a high interaction with service value chain activities *Obtain/build* and *Design and transition*, a medium interaction with *Plan* and *Improve*, and a low interaction with *Engage* and *Deliver and support*.

### 5.2.14  Service desk

*All*

The **purpose** of the service desk practice is to capture demand for incident resolution and service requests.

It should also be the entry point and *single point of contact* for the service provider with all of its users. The service desk is a practice, and not just a function. It involves all four dimensions of service management (Figure 4).

The **service desk** is the point of communication between the service provider and all of its users. The **service desk** *practice* involves capturing demand for incident resolution and service requests.

Service desks provide a clear path for users to report issues, queries, and requests. They may use various **channels for access**, including:

- phone calls, including interactive voice response (IVR), conference calls, voice recognition
- service portals and mobile applications, supported by service and request catalogues, and knowledge bases
- chat, through live chat and chatbots
- email for logging and updating, and for follow-up surveys and confirmations
- walk-in service desks, when a physical presence is required
- messaging, for broadcasting notifications, for contacting specific stakeholder groups, and supporting requests from users
- social media and discussion forums for contacting the service provider and for peer-to-peer support

With increased automation[6], service desks provide more **self-service** logging and resolution directly via online portals and mobile applications ('shift left'). Consequently, the service desk now has reduced phone contact, less low-level work, and a greater ability to focus on excellent CX when personal contact is needed.

The service desk sees to it that all issues, queries, and requests are acknowledged, classified, owned, and actioned, in close collaboration with all other teams in the organization, internal as well as external.

The service desk is the empathetic and informed link between the service provider and its users, focusing on people and business and not just on technical issues. It has a major influence on UX and how the service provider is perceived by the users (customer satisfaction). Service desk staff need to demonstrate excellent customer service skills such as:

- empathy
- effective communication

---

6   Artificial intelligence (AI), robotic process automation (RPA), chatbots

- emotional intelligence
- understanding business priorities

**Understanding the business is the key skill**: being able to fully understand and diagnose a specific incident, issue or request, in terms of business priority and relevance, and to take appropriate action to get this resolved.

Service desks may be centralized, tangible teams, or they may be **virtual service desks**, with agents working from any location. These virtual service desks in particular will require more sophisticated technologies, including:

- intelligent telephony systems, with computer-telephony integration (CTI), interactive voice-response systems (IVR), and automatic call distribution  *5/a*
- workflow systems for routing and escalation
- workforce management and resource planning systems
- a knowledge base
- call recording and quality control
- remote access tools *– fix user's PC.*
- dashboard and monitoring tools
- configuration management systems *, what is affected*

Service desks may have a limited **support window** where service coverage is available.

The practice has a high interaction with service value chain activities *Engage* and *Deliver and support*, a medium interaction with *Improve* and *Design and transition*, and a low interaction with *Obtain/build*. There is no significant interaction with the service value chain activity *Plan*.

*[handwritten in left margin: So Serve Design dies and set prformance lengths? AU]*

## 5.2.15 Service level management *[handwritten: AU]*

The **purpose** of the service level management practice is to set clear, business-based targets for service performance, so that the delivery of a service can be properly assessed, monitored, and managed against these targets.

This practice involves the definition, documentation, and active management of service levels.

> *Service level*: One or more metrics that define expected or achieved service quality.

To provide end-to-end visibility of the organization's services for multiple stakeholders, service level management provides:

- a **shared view** of the services and target service levels with customers
- relevant **metrics** for the identified services
- **service reviews** to ensure that current services continue to meet the needs of the organization and its customers
- information on **service performance** issues, so that appropriate interventions can be taken

Service providers and service consumers can agree on the services, and document this in service level agreements (SLAs).

> *Service level agreement*: A documented agreement between a service provider and a customer that identifies both the services required and the expected level of service.

It is important that SLAs align the customer's and the provider's expectations. SLAs should relate to:

- defined and measurable **services**, as described in the service catalogue
- defined **outcomes**, expressed in terms of the value for the customer

*[handwritten: A result, not output.]*

They must be simply written and easy to understand, and use, for all involved parties. The measurement, based on SLAs, should be meaningful, reflecting the actual CX and customer satisfaction. If a service level metric indicates a job well done (availability met the agreed 99.9%) but the customer is not satisfied (the 0.1% unavailability happened to be right in the middle of a major business campaign), then the metric doesn't reflect the expected value. False metrics like these would lead to a **watermelon effect** (green on the outside, but red inside), which should be avoided.

Service level management is all about relationships. It builds on relationship management, business liaison, supplier management and business analysis skills and competencies. It requires *engaging* with the actual needs and requirements of the customer and *listening* to them in order to build a trustful relationship. The service provider should understand the customer's business in detail, through an active attitude, using various communication techniques and sources of customer feedback from surveys and measurements.

The practice has a high interaction with service value chain activities *Plan* and *Engage,* and a medium interaction with *Improve, Obtain/build, Design and transition* and *Deliver and support.*

## 5.2.16  Service request management             All

The **purpose** of the service request management practice is to support the agreed quality of a service by handling all predefined, user-initiated service requests in an effective and user-friendly manner.

so BAU nd. Problems

Service requests are a normal part of service delivery and are not a failure or degradation of service, which are handled as incidents.

*Service request:* A request from a user or a user's authorized representative that initiates a service action which has been agreed as a normal part of service delivery

Service requests are pre-agreed with the customer in terms of what they deliver and when. This means they are likely to be formalized and handled in predefined procedures. These may be simple or complex, but they are always **standardized**.

If possible, procedures for service requests should be **automated**. The service provider should continually seek options to improve the fulfillment of (automated) service requests.

A service catalogue may hold many of these service requests, to streamline their fulfillment and to set user expectations. Some service requests may require specific authorization, others may be initiated by (all) users in self-service portals.

Handling of service requests follows a straightforward procedure, covering initiation, approval and fulfillment. The fulfillment may include changes to services or their components; usually these are *standard changes*.

Service requests may include various activities, like routine service delivery actions, requests for information, requests for provision of a resource or service, requests for access to a resource or service, feedback, compliments, and complaints. If a service request is actually an *incident* call or a *change request*, procedures should be in place to redirect the call to the adequate practice.

The practice has a high interaction with service value chain activities *Engage* and *Deliver and support*, a medium interaction with *Obtain/build* and *Design and transition,* and low interaction with *Improve*. There is no significant interaction with the service value chain activity *Plan*.

### 5.2.17 Service validation and testing

> The **purpose** of the service validation and testing practice is to ensure that new or changed products and services meet defined requirements.

Service validation focuses on establishing deployment and release management **acceptance criteria**, which are verified through testing. Acceptance criteria can be either utility- or warranty-focused, and are defined through understanding customer, regulatory, business, risk management, and security requirements.

A **test strategy** defines an overall approach to testing. It can apply to any set of components. The test strategy is based on the service acceptance criteria.

**Test types** include *utility/functional tests* (unit, system, integration, and regression tests) and *warranty/non-functional tests* (testing performance and capacity, security, compliance, operational functions, warranty requirements, and user acceptance).

The practice has a high interaction with service value chain activities *Obtain/build* and *Design and transition*, a medium interaction with *Improve*, and low interaction with *Engage* and *Deliver and support*. There is no significant interaction with the service value chain activity *Plan*.

## ■ 5.3 TECHNICAL MANAGEMENT PRACTICES

ITIL 4 describes three technical management practices.

The ITIL 4 Foundation exam requires that candidates can recall the **purpose** of one technical management practice, namely:
■ deployment management

The remaining two practices are not examined.

### 5.3.1 Deployment management

> The **purpose** of the deployment management practice is to move new or changed hardware, software, documentation, processes, or any other component to live environments, or to environments for testing or staging.

Deployment management works closely with release management and change control. It may use several approaches, including:

- **phased deployment**, when new or updated components are deployed to parts of the production environment at a time
- **continuous delivery**, when components are integrated, tested and deployed whenever they are needed
- **big bang deployment**, when all components are delivered to all target environments at once
- **pull deployment**, where users deploy the objects themselves from a controlled depository

Deployment management refers to *infrastructure* as well as *software*. Components that are available for deployment should be maintained in one or more secure locations (*definitive media libraries* or *definitive hardware stores*).

Deployment can be supported by automation tools e.g. for deploying client software.

Communication around deployments is part of release management. It is essential that the organization is aware of all deployments so that a controlled environment can be maintained.

The practice has a high interaction with service value chain activities *Obtain/build* and *Design and transition*, and medium interaction with *Improve*. There is no significant interaction with the service value chain activities *Plan*, *Engage*, and *Deliver and support*.

### 5.3.2 Infrastructure and platform management

The **purpose** of the infrastructure and platform management practice is to oversee the infrastructure and platforms used by an organization.

IT infrastructure is the physical and/or virtual technology resources, such as servers, storage, networks, client hardware, middleware, and operating systems software, that provide the environments needed to deliver IT services.

This includes any CI a customer uses to access the service or consume a product, and also the facilities that are required to develop, test, deliver, monitor, manage and support IT services.

Infrastructure and platform management may also include the buildings and facilities an organization uses to run its IT infrastructure.

IT infrastructure and platforms are now often built using cloud technology. Consumers can get processing, storage, and/or any other computing resources without having to control the underlying infrastructure. Cloud service models include:

- **software as a service** (SaaS), offering the *use* of cloud-based applications that run on infrastructure provided and managed by the cloud provider
- **platform as a service** *(PaaS)*, offering the *management* of cloud-based applications that run on infrastructure provided and managed by the cloud provider
- **infrastructure as a service** (IaaS), offering an *application management environment* for cloud-based applications without having to run the underlying infrastructure provided and managed by the cloud provider

Every service model can be deployed in several ways, including *private cloud*, *public cloud*, or *community cloud*. A *hybrid cloud* is a composition of two or more of these cloud infrastructures.

The practice has a high interaction with service value chain activities *Obtain/build* and *Design and transition,* a medium interaction with *Plan* and *Deliver and support,* a low interaction with *Improve.* There is no significant interaction with the service value chain activity *Engage.*

### 5.3.3  Software development and management

> The **purpose** of the software development and management practice is to ensure that applications meet internal and external stakeholder needs, in terms of functionality, reliability, maintainability, compliance, and auditability.

The term 'software' can be used to describe anything from a single program (or suite of programs) to larger constructs (such as an operating system, an operating environment, or a database) on which various smaller application programs, processes, or workflows can run.

The practice applies to any size of software or combination of programs, desktop applications, mobile apps, embedded (machine) software, websites, or any other format of software.

Software development and management is a key practice in every modern IT organization. It may apply waterfall or Agile methods, DevOps, or any other approach. Its activities cover the entire software lifecycle, from ideation, design, development, testing, deployment, and operation, up to retirement.

The practice has a high interaction with service value chain activity *Obtain/build,* a medium interaction with *Improve* and *Design and transition,* and a low interaction with *Plan* and *Deliver and support.* There is no significant interaction with the service value chain activity *Engage.*

# ■ 5.4 RELATIONSHIPS BETWEEN PRACTICES AND SERVICE VALUE CHAIN ACTIVITIES

As explained in this chapter, the service value chain activities may use any combination of ITIL practices to achieve their goals. In turn, the ITIL practices may support any of the service value chain activities. Not each practice is designed to support each activity in the same way or intensity. The next six figures demonstrate how each activity in the service value chain relates to each of the 34 ITIL practices, in a *heatmap*.

The three practice categories are formatted differently. Within each interaction level, each practice category can be distinguished from the others.

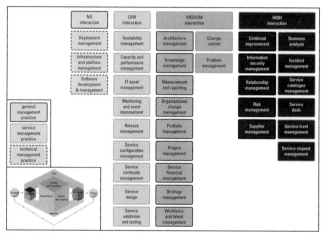

Figure 12. The practice heatmap of Engage

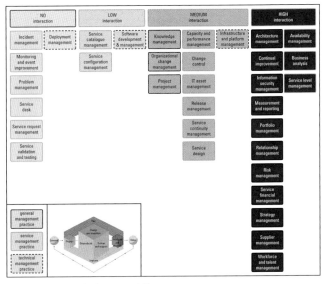

Figure 13. The practice heatmap of Plan

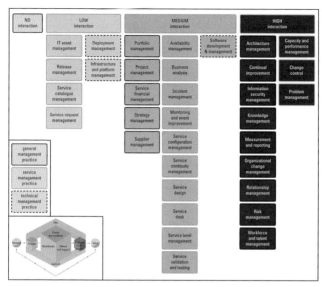

Figure 14. The practice heatmap of Improve

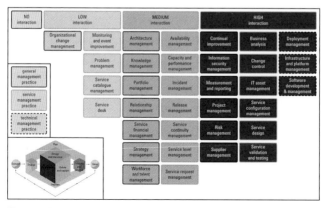

Figure 15. The practice heatmap of Obtain/build

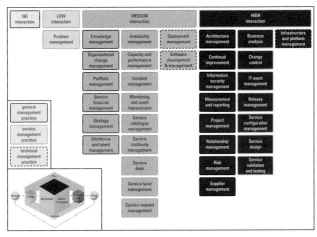

Figure 16.  The practice heatmap of Design and transition

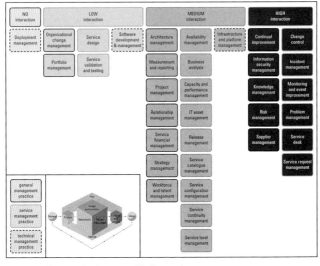

Figure 17.  The practice heatmap of Deliver and support

# 6 The ITIL 4 Foundation Exam

## ■ 6.1 PURPOSE

The purpose of the ITIL 4 Foundation qualification is to introduce candidates to the management of modern IT-enabled services, to provide them with an understanding of the common language and key concepts, and to show them how they can improve their work and the work of their organization with ITIL 4 guidance.

Furthermore, the qualification will provide the candidate with an understanding of the ITIL 4 service management framework and how it has evolved to adopt modern technologies and ways of working.

The purpose of the ITIL 4 Foundation examination is to assess whether the candidate can demonstrate sufficient recall and understanding of the ITIL 4 service management framework to be awarded the ITIL 4 Foundation qualification. The ITIL 4 Foundation qualification is a prerequisite for the ITIL 4 higher level qualifications, which assess the ability to apply the concepts, and the ability to understand relevant parts of the ITIL framework in context. The detailed requirements for the ITIL 4 Foundation examination are documented in the syllabus. This syllabus can be downloaded from the AXELOS website.

## ■ 6.2   CONDITIONS

Candidates are allowed up to 60 minutes to take the exam. Candidates that take the exam in a language that is not their native or working language may be awarded 15 minutes extra time.

The ITIL 4 Foundation exam is a closed book exam, meaning that you are not allowed to have any material at hand during the exam, apart from the examination materials.

## ■ 6.3   QUESTION TYPES

All questions have four options. The candidate should select the correct answer. There is only one correct answer for each question.

Questions follow one of the following types:
- **standard**: select the right answer from 4 options
- **missing word**: select a missing word in a sentence, from a list of 4 options
- **list**: select a combination of 2 correct items from a list
- **negative question**: select the right answer from 4 options, for a negative statement (e.g. "what is not….")

Negative questions are only used, as an exception, where part of the learning outcome is to know that something is not done or should not occur.

## ■ 6.4   SCORING

The exam has 40 questions. Each question is allocated 1 mark. Candidates pass the exam if they score 26 marks or more.

There are nine questions at Bloom's level 1 ('recall'/'define'), and 31 questions at Bloom's level 2 ('describe'/'explain').

Each candidate gets a standard number of questions for each learning outcome:

- understand the key service concepts: **five questions**
- understand how the ITIL guiding principles can help an organization adopt and adapt service management: **six questions**
- understand the four dimensions of service management: **two questions**
- understand the purpose and components of the ITIL service value system: **one question** *On one!*
- understand the activities of the service value chain, and how they interconnect: **two questions**
- know the purpose and key terms of 15 ITIL practices: **seven questions**
- understand 7 ITIL practices: **17 questions**

*} 24 above!*

## ■ 6.5   PREPARATION

Candidates for the ITIL 4 Foundation exam are advised to take either a classroom training course or an e-training course. Taking a training course is not mandatory, but it will enhance a candidate's chances of passing the exam.

Candidates may also use this pocket guide as a preparation for the exam, or read the ITIL 4 Foundation publication.

## ■ 6.6   QUALIFICATION SCHEME

ITIL 4 Foundation is the entry level certification, demonstrating a general awareness of the key elements, concepts and terminology used in ITIL 4.

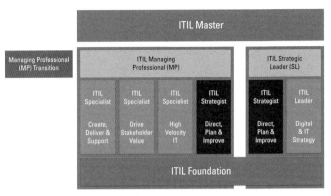

Figure 18. The ITIL 4 Certification Scheme

The ITIL 4 Certification Scheme (shown in Figure 18) is designed to be backwards compatible with ITIL v3. It comprises of the following modules:

- ITIL 4 Foundation
- ITIL Specialist modules:
  - Create, Deliver and Support
  - Drive Stakeholder Value
  - High Velocity IT
- ITIL Strategist: Direct, Plan & Improve
- ITIL Leader: Digital & IT Strategy
- ITIL Managing Professional Transition

The ITIL Leader: Digital and IT Strategy module mandates three years of managerial experience as a prerequisite, along with completion of ITIL 4 Foundation.

To obtain the designation of **ITIL Managing Professional** (ITIL MP), the candidate must complete the following modules:

- ITIL 4 Foundation (prerequisite for the other modules)
- All three ITIL Specialist modules:

- Create, Deliver and Support
- Drive Stakeholder Value
- High Velocity IT
- ITIL Strategist: Direct, Plan and Improve

Candidates who have already been awarded ITIL Expert or ITIL Master under the ITIL v3 regime, or those with 17 credits or more from ITIL v3, may use the *Managing Professional Transition* module to gain the ITIL MP designation. The Transition module covers the core elements from the ITIL Managing Professional stream. It has a mandatory training element and exam, enabling v3 candidates to transition their existing designations into the new ITIL 4 certification scheme.

To obtain the designation of **ITIL Strategic Leader** (ITIL SL), the candidate must complete the following modules:
- ITIL 4 Foundation (prerequisite for the other modules)
- ITIL Leader: Digital and IT Strategy
- ITIL Strategist: Direct, Plan and Improve

Candidates who achieve both designations are eligible for assessment to become an **ITIL Master**.

# 7 Differences with previous ITIL versions

ITIL has taken a great step forward from its previous versions. ITIL 4 applies a modern perception of service management from a customer-centric perspective. It positions service management according to a Service-Dominant logic, where value is no longer perceived as **value-in-exchange** but as **value-in-use**, and where value is co-created by providers and their consumers, in a joint effort.

This is expressed in the ITIL **service value system** (SVS) and in the concept of the ITIL **service value chain** (service value chain), using **value streams** for delivering any contribution to the creation of value.

In ITIL v3, the service provider domain was built with the following elements:
- people
- processes
- products (services, technology and tools)
- partners (suppliers, manufacturers and vendors)

In ITIL 4, the service provider domain is still constructed from similar elements:
- organizations and people
- value streams and processes

- information and technology
- partners and suppliers

The ITIL v3 service lifecycle structure, describing a set of core processes for each lifecycle stage in a rather redundant structure, has been replaced with the concept of the service value chain. This service value chain is composed of similar elements as the service lifecycle structure, but it can be used in a much more flexible way. It allows the service provider to create value streams that are composed of any combination of the elements of the service value chain, in any iterative manner.

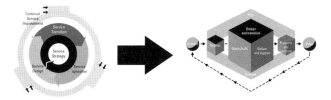

Figure 19.  The transition of the ITIL v3 lifecycle to the ITIL 4 service value chain

Each of the value chain activities can be supported by many practices. They also can be combined in multiple service value streams, according to the needs of the organization. The set of 26 *processes*, four Service Delivery *activities*, 11 Service Operation *activities*, and four Service Operation *functions*, as defined in ITIL v3, has been redefined into three sets of **practices**, now covering 34 ITIL practices for service management:

- **14 general management practices**, adopted and adapted for service management from general business management domains
- **17 service management practices**, developed in service management and ITSM industries
- **3 technical management practices** that have been uplifted from being service management *functions*, to become more generic, technical *practices* that are available to the entire organization

The ITIL 4 Foundation exam covers 24 questions on these practices, and 16 questions on the rest of the material, covering the key concepts, the guiding principles, the four dimensions, the service value system and the service value chain activities. As the majority of the exam questions relate to practices, exam candidates should carefully study the updated set of ITIL practices.

ITIL 4's redefined use of the terms **practice** and **process** has some serious implications. A process is still defined as a specific sequence of activities, but in ITIL 4, incident management, capacity management, problem management, release management etc. are no longer defined as processes: instead they are now considered to be **practices**. In fact, the ITIL Foundation, ITIL 4 Edition does not provide a list of processes any more. This reassessment of the term *process* has some implications for the service value chain: practices can be applied to any value stream in the service value chain, unlike the way in which the previous ITIL processes (or rather: practices) were allocated to specific phases of the ITIL Service Lifecycle to a certain degree.

ITIL 4 still refers to various processes, e.g. a risk management process, an information security incident management process, a control review and audit process, an identity and access management process, and various configuration management processes, but these are not specifically described in the ITIL 4 Foundation material. It is common to have different processes for different environments within one practice. For example, there may be one process for the deployment of client application software, and a completely different process for the deployment of server operating system patches.

■ **7.1   CHANGES TO THE LIST OF PROCESSES/PRACTICES**

Readers with a knowledge of ITIL v3 will benefit from understanding how the ITIL v3 processes, activities, and functions, have transformed into the

34 ITIL 4 practices. Although the ITIL 4 Foundation publication doesn't provide details about the explicit evolution from ITIL v3 to ITIL 4, there are serious differences in the listing of processes/practices.

A number of ITIL v3 processes haven't changed: these are listed over both columns in Table 1, but now as ITIL 4 practices.

However, most ITIL v3 processes have been redefined to some degree:

■ Some ITIL v3 processes have been split into two separate ITIL 4 practices.

■ Some ITIL v3 processes have been combined into a single ITIL 4 practice.

■ Some ITIL v3 common activities have been upgraded to an ITIL 4 practice.

| ITIL v3 phase | ITIL v3 process | ITIL 4 practice |
|---|---|---|
| Service strategy | Strategy management for IT services | Strategy management |
| Service strategy | Service portfolio management | Portfolio management |
| Service strategy | Financial management for IT services | Service financial management |
| Service strategy | Business relationship management | Relationship management |
| | | Business analysis |
| Service strategy | Demand management | Capacity and performance management |
| Service design | Capacity management | |
| Service design | Design coordination | Service design |
| Service design | Service catalogue management | |
| Service design | Service level management | |
| Service design | Availability management | |
| Service design | IT service continuity management | Service continuity management |
| Service design | Information security management | Information security management |
| Service operation | Access management | |

| ITIL v3 phase | ITIL v3 process | ITIL 4 practice |
|---|---|---|
| Service design | Supplier management | |
| Service transition | Transition planning and support | Change control |
| Service transition | Change management | |
| Service transition | Change evaluation | |
| Service transition | Service asset and configuration management | Service configuration management |
| Service transition | | IT asset management |
| Service transition | Release and deployment management | Release management |
| Service transition | | Deployment management |
| Service transition | Service validation and testing | |
| Service transition | Knowledge management | |
| Service operation | Event management | Monitoring and event management |
| Common operation activities | Monitoring and control | |
| Service operation | Incident management | |
| Service operation | Request fulfillment | Service request management |
| Service operation | Problem management | |
| Service operation | The function Servicedesk | Servicedesk |
| Continual service improvement | The seven-step improvement process (the CSI improvement process) | Continual improvement |
| Various, or not explicitly covered activities or practices | ITIL v3 common service operation activities, including measurement and reporting, IT Operations, Print and output management, Network management, Storage and archive, etc., or activities and practices that were not explicitly covered | Measurement and reporting |
| | | Project management |
| | | Infrastructure and platform management |
| | | Software development and management |
| | | Risk management |
| | | Organizational change management |
| | | Workforce and talent management |
| | | Architecture management |

Table 1. An interpretation of the conversion of ITIL v3 processes and activities to ITIL 4 practices

Exam candidates should only study the practices at the level of information that is provided in chapter 5.

# 8 Glossary

Note: the glossary contains all terms as presented in the official ITIL 4 Glossary. The list includes many terms that are *not examinable*. Unlike in the rest of this pocket guide, to aid in readability the glossary is formatted in standard, black font.

**Acceptance criteria**: A list of minimum requirements that a service or service component must meet for it to be acceptable to key stakeholders.

**Agile**: An umbrella term for a collection of frameworks and techniques that together enable teams and individuals to work in a way that is typified by collaboration, prioritization, iterative and incremental delivery, and time boxing.
There are several specific methods (or frameworks) that are classified as Agile, such as Scrum, Lean, and Kanban.

**Architecture management practice**: The practice of providing an understanding of all the different elements that make up an organization and how those elements relate to one another.

**Asset register**: A database or list of assets, capturing key attributes such as ownership and financial value.

**Availability**: The ability of an IT service or other configuration item to perform its agreed function when required.

**Availability management practice**: The practice of ensuring that services deliver agreed levels of availability to meet the needs of customers and users.

**Baseline**: A report or metric that serves as a starting point against which progress or change can be assessed.

**Best practice**: A way of working that has been proven to be successful by multiple organizations.

**Big data**: The use of very large volumes of structured and unstructured data from a variety of sources to gain new insights.

**Business analysis practice**: The practice of analyzing a business or some element of a business, defining its needs and recommending solutions to address these needs and/or solve a business problem, and create value for stakeholders.

**Business case:** A justification for expenditure of organizational resources, providing information about costs, benefits, options, risks, and issues.

**Business impact analysis** (BIA): A key activity in the practice of service continuity management that identifies vital business functions and their dependencies.

**Business relationship manager** (BRM): A role responsible for maintaining good relationships with one or more customers.

**Call**: An interaction (e.g. a telephone call) with the service desk.
A call could result in an incident or a service request being logged.

**Call/contact center**: An organization or business unit that handles large numbers of incoming and outgoing calls and other interactions.

**Capability**: The ability of an organization, person, process, application, configuration item, or IT service to carry out an activity.

**Capacity and performance management practice**: The practice of ensuring that services achieve agreed and expected performance levels, satisfying current and future demand in a cost-effective way.

**Capacity planning**: The activity of creating a plan that manages resources to meet demand for services.

**Change**: The addition, modification, or removal of anything that could have a direct or indirect effect on services.

**Change authority**: A person or group responsible for authorizing a change.

**Change control practice**: The practice of ensuring that risks are properly assessed, authorizing changes to proceed and managing a change schedule in order to maximize the number of successful IT changes.

**Change model**: A repeatable approach to the management of a particular type of change.

**Change schedule**: A calendar that shows planned and historical changes.

**Charging**: The activity that assigns a price for services.

**Cloud computing**: A model for enabling on-demand network access to a shared pool of configurable computing resources that can be rapidly provided with minimal management effort or provider interaction.

**Compliance**: The act of ensuring that a standard or set of guidelines is followed, or that proper, consistent accounting or other practices are being employed.

**Confidentiality**: A security objective that ensures information is not made available or disclosed to unauthorized entities.

**Configuration**: An arrangement of configuration items (CIs) or other resources that work together to deliver a product or service.
Can also be used to describe the parameter settings for one or more CIs.

**Configuration item** (CI): Any component that needs to be managed in order to deliver an IT service.

**Configuration management database** (CMDB): A database used to store configuration records throughout their lifecycle.
The CMDB also maintains the relationships between configuration records.

**Configuration management system** (CMS): A set of tools, data, and information that is used to support service configuration management.

**Configuration record:** A record containing the details of a configuration item (CI).
Each configuration record documents the lifecycle of a single CI.
Configuration records are stored in a configuration management database.

**Continual improvement practice**: The practice of aligning an organization's practices and services with changing business needs through the ongoing identification and improvement of all elements involved in the effective management of products and services.

**Continuous integration/continuous delivery**: An integrated set of practices and tools used to merge developers' code, build and test the resulting software, and package it so that it is ready for deployment.

**Control**: The means of managing a risk, ensuring that a business objective is achieved, or that a process is followed.

**Cost**: The amount of money spent on a specific activity or resource.

**Cost center**: A business unit or project to which costs are assigned.

**Critical success factor** (CSF): A necessary precondition for the achievement of intended results.

**Culture**: A set of values that is shared by a group of people, including expectations about how people should behave, ideas, beliefs, and practices.

**Customer**: A person who defines the requirements for a service and takes responsibility for the outcomes of service consumption.

**Customer experience** (CX): The sum of functional and emotional interactions with a service and service provider as perceived by a service consumer.

**Dashboard**: A real-time graphical representation of data.

**Deliver and support**: The value chain activity that ensures services are delivered and supported according to agreed specifications and stakeholders' expectations.

**Demand**: Input to the service value system based on opportunities and needs from internal and external stakeholders.

**Deployment**: The movement of any service component into any environment.

**Deployment management practice**: The practice of moving new or changed hardware, software, documentation, processes, or any other service component to live environments.

**Design and transition**: The value chain activity that ensures products and services continually meet stakeholder expectations for quality, costs, and time to market.

**Design thinking**: A practical and human-centered approach used by product and service designers to solve complex problems and find practical and creative solutions that meet the needs of an organization and its customers.

**Development environment**: An environment used to create or modify IT services or applications.

**DevOps**: An organizational culture that aims to improve the flow of value to customers. DevOps focuses on culture, automation, Lean, measurement, and sharing (CALMS).

**Digital transformation**: The evolution of traditional business models to meet the needs of highly empowered customers, with technology playing an enabling role.

**Disaster recovery plans**: A set of clearly defined plans related to how an organization will recover from a disaster as well as return to a pre-disaster condition, considering the four dimensions of service management.

**Driver**: Something that influences strategy, objectives, or requirements.

**Effectiveness**: A measure of whether the objectives of a practice, service or activity have been achieved.

**Efficiency**: A measure of whether the right amount of resources have been used by a practice, service, or activity.

**Emergency change**: A change that must be introduced as soon as possible.

**Engage**: The value chain activity that provides a good understanding of stakeholder needs, transparency, continual engagement, and good relationships with all stakeholders.

**Environment**: A subset of the IT infrastructure that is used for a particular purpose, for example a live environment or test environment.
Can also mean the external conditions that influence or affect something.

**Error**: A flaw or vulnerability that may cause incidents.

**Error control**: Problem management activities used to manage known errors.

**Escalation**: The act of sharing awareness or transferring ownership of an issue or work item.

 **Event**: Any change of state that has significance for the management of a service or other configuration item.

**External customer**: A customer who works for an organization other than the service provider.

**Failure**: A loss of ability to operate to specification, or to deliver the required output or outcome.

**Feedback loop**: A technique whereby the outputs of one part of a system are used as inputs to the same part of the system.

**Four dimensions of service management**: The four perspectives that are critical to the effective and efficient facilitation of value for customers and other stakeholders in the form of products and services.

**Governance**: The means by which an organization is directed and controlled.

**Identity**: A unique name that is used to identify and grant system access rights to a user, person, or role.

**Improve**: The value chain activity that ensures continual improvement of products, services, and practices across all value chain activities and the four dimensions of service management.

**Incident**: An unplanned interruption to a service or reduction in the quality of a service.

**Incident management practice**: The practice of minimizing the negative impact of incidents by restoring normal service operation as quickly as possible.

**Information and technology**: One of the four dimensions of service management.
It includes the information and knowledge used to deliver services, and the information and technologies used to manage all aspects of the service value system.

**Information security management practice**: The practice of protecting an organization by understanding and managing risks to the confidentiality, integrity, and availability of information.

**Information security policy**: The policy that governs an organization's approach to information security management.

**Infrastructure and platform management practice**: The practice of overseeing the infrastructure and platforms used by an organization. This enables the monitoring of technology solutions available, including solutions from third parties.

**Integrity**: A security objective that ensures information is only modified by authorized personnel and activities.

**Internal customer**: A customer who works for the same organization as the service provider.

**Internet of Things**: The interconnection of devices via the internet that were not traditionally thought of as IT assets, but now include embedded computing capability and network connectivity.

**IT asset**: Any financially valuable component that can contribute to the delivery of an IT product or service.

**IT asset management practice**: The practice of planning and managing the full lifecycle of all IT assets.

**IT infrastructure**: All of the hardware, software, networks, and facilities that are required to develop, test, deliver, monitor, manage, and support IT services.

**IT service**: A service based on the use of information technology.

**ITIL**: Best-practice guidance for IT service management.

**ITIL guiding principles**: Recommendations that can guide an organization in all circumstances, regardless of changes in its goals, strategies, type of work, or management structure.

**ITIL service value chain**: An operating model for service providers that covers all the key activities required to effectively manage products and services.

**Kanban**: A method for visualizing work, identifying potential blockages and resource conflicts, and managing work in progress.

**Key performance indicator** (KPI): An important metric used to evaluate the success in meeting an objective.

**Knowledge management practice**: The practice of maintaining and improving the effective, efficient, and convenient use of information and knowledge across an organization.

**Known error**: A problem that has been analyzed but has not been resolved.

**Lean**: An approach that focuses on improving workflows by maximizing value through the elimination of waste.

**Lifecycle**: The full set of stages, transitions, and associated statuses in the life of a service, product, practice, or other entity.

**Live**: Refers to a service or other configuration item operating in the live environment.

**Live environment**: A controlled environment used in the delivery of IT services to service consumers.

**Maintainability**: The ease with which a service or other entity can be repaired or modified.

**Major incident**: An incident with significant business impact, requiring an immediate coordinated resolution.

**Management system**: Interrelated or interacting elements that establish policy and objectives and enable the achievement of those objectives.

**Maturity**: A measure of the reliability, efficiency and effectiveness of an organization, practice, or process.

**Mean time between failures** (MTBF): A metric of how frequently a service or other configuration item fails.

**Mean time to restore service** (MTRS): A metric of how quickly a service is restored after a failure.

**Measurement and reporting practice**: The practice of supporting good decision-making and continual improvement by decreasing levels of uncertainty.

**Metric**: A measurement or calculation that is monitored or reported for management and improvement.

**Minimum viable product** (MVP): A product with just enough features to satisfy early customers, and to provide feedback for future product development.

**Mission statement**: A short but complete description of the overall purpose and intentions of an organization. It states what is to be achieved, but not how this should be done.

**Model**: A representation of a system, practice, process, service, or other entity that is used to understand and predict its behavior and relationships.

**Modelling**: The activity of creating, maintaining, and utilizing models.

**Monitoring**: Repeated observation of a system, practice, process, service, or other entity to detect events and to ensure that the current status is known.

**Monitoring and event management practice**: The practice of systematically observing services and service components, and recording and reporting selected changes of state identified as events.

**Obtain/build:** The value chain activity that ensures service components are available when and where they are needed, and that they meet agreed specifications.

**Operation**: The routine running and management of an activity, product, service, or other configuration item.

**Operational technology**: The hardware and software solutions that detect or cause changes in physical processes through direct monitoring and/or control of physical devices such as valves, pumps, etc.

**Organization**: A person or a group of people that has its own functions with responsibilities, authorities, and relationships to achieve its objectives.

**Organizational change management practice**: The practice of ensuring that changes in an organization are smoothly and successfully implemented and that lasting benefits are achieved by managing the human aspects of the changes.

**Organizational resilience**: The ability of an organization to anticipate, prepare for, respond to, and adapt to unplanned external influences.

**Organizational velocity**: The speed, effectiveness, and efficiency with which an organization operates.
Organizational velocity influences time to market, quality, safety, costs, and risks.

**Organizations and people**: One of the four dimensions of service management.
It ensures that the way an organization is structured and managed, as well as its roles, responsibilities, and systems of authority and communication, is well defined and supports its overall strategy and operating model.

**Outcome**: A result for a stakeholder enabled by one or more outputs.

**Output**: A tangible or intangible deliverable of an activity.

**Outsourcing**: The process of having external suppliers provide products and services that were previously provided internally.

**Partners and suppliers**: One of the four dimensions of service management.
It encompasses the relationships an organization has with other organizations that are involved in the design, development, deployment, delivery, support, and/or continual improvement of services.

**Partnership**: A relationship between two organizations that involves working closely together to achieve common goals and objectives.

**Performance**: A measure of what is achieved or delivered by a system, person, team, practice, or service.

**Pilot**: A test implementation of a service with a limited scope in a live environment.

**Plan**: The value chain activity that ensures a shared understanding of the vision, current status, and improvement direction for all four dimensions and all products and services across an organization.

**Policy**: Formally documented management expectations and intentions, used to direct decisions and activities.

**Portfolio management practice**: The practice of ensuring that an organization has the right mix of programs, projects, products, and services to execute its strategy within its funding and resource constraints.

**Post-implementation review** (PIR): A review after the implementation of a change, to evaluate success and identify opportunities for improvement.

**Practice**: A set of organizational resources designed for performing work or accomplishing an objective.

**Problem**: A cause, or potential cause, of one or more incidents.

**Problem management practice**: The practice of reducing the likelihood and impact of incidents by identifying actual and potential causes of incidents, and managing workarounds and known errors.

**Procedure**: A documented way to carry out an activity or a process.

**Process**: A set of interrelated or interacting activities that transform inputs into outputs.
A process takes one or more defined inputs and turns them into defined outputs. Processes define the sequence of actions and their dependencies.

**Product**: A configuration of an organization's resources designed to offer value for a consumer.

**Production environment**. See live environment.

**Program**: A set of related projects and activities, and an organization structure created to direct and oversee them.

**Project**: A temporary structure that is created for the purpose of delivering one or more outputs (or products) according to an agreed business case.

**Project management practice**: The practice of ensuring that all an organization's projects are successfully delivered.

**Quick win**: An improvement that is expected to provide a return on investment in a short period of time with relatively small cost and effort.

**Record**: A document stating results achieved and providing evidence of activities performed.

**Recovery**: The activity of returning a configuration item to normal operation after a failure.

**Recovery point objective** (RPO): The point to which information used by an activity must be restored to enable the activity to operate on resumption.

**Recovery time objective** (RTO:) The maximum acceptable period of time following a service disruption that can elapse before the lack of business functionality severely impacts the organization.

**Relationship management practice**: The practice of establishing and nurturing links between an organization and its stakeholders at strategic and tactical levels.

**Release**: A version of a service or other configuration item, or a collection of configuration items, that is made available for use.

**Release management practice**: The practice of making new and changed services and features available for use.

**Reliability**: The ability of a product, service, or other configuration item to perform its intended function for a specified period of time or number of cycles.

**Request catalogue**: A view of the service catalogue, providing details on service requests for existing and new services, which is made available for the user.

**Request for change** (RFC): A description of a proposed change used to initiate change control.

**Resolution**: The action of solving an incident or problem.

**Resource**: A person, or other entity, that is required for the execution of an activity or the achievement of an objective.

**Retire**: The act of permanently withdrawing a product, service, or other configuration item from use.

**Risk**: A possible event that could cause harm or loss, or make it more difficult to achieve objectives.
Can also be defined as uncertainty of outcome, and can be used in the context of measuring the probability of positive outcomes as well as negative outcomes.

**Risk assessment**: An activity to identify, analyze, and evaluate risks.

**Risk management practice**: The practice of ensuring that an organization understands and effectively handles risks.

**Service**: A means of enabling value co-creation by facilitating outcomes that customers want to achieve, without the customer having to manage specific costs and risks.

**Service architecture**: A view of all the services provided by an organization. It includes interactions between the services, and service models that describe the structure and dynamics of each service.

**Service catalogue**: Structured information about all the services and service offerings of a service provider, relevant for a specific target audience.

**Service catalogue management practice**: The practice of providing a single source of consistent information on all services and service offerings, and ensuring that it is available to the relevant audience.

**Service configuration management practice**: The practice of ensuring that accurate and reliable information about the configuration of services, and the configuration items that support them, is available when and where needed.

**Service consumption**: Activities performed by an organization to consume services.
It includes the management of the consumer's resources needed to use the service, service actions performed by users, and the receiving (acquiring) of goods (if required).

**Service continuity management practice**: The practice of ensuring that service availability and performance are maintained at a sufficient level in the event of a disaster.

**Service design practice**: The practice of designing products and services that are fit for purpose, fit for use, and that can be delivered by the organization and its ecosystem.

**Service desk**: The point of communication between the service provider and all its users.

**Service desk practice**: The practice of capturing demand for incident resolution and service requests.

**Service financial management practice**: The practice of supporting an organization's strategies and plans for service management by ensuring that the organization's financial resources and investments are being used effectively.

**Service level**: A set of measurable parameters defining expected or achieved service quality.

**Service level agreement** (SLA): A documented agreement between a service provider and a customer that identifies both services required and the expected level of service.

**Service level management practice**: The practice of setting clear business-based targets for service performance so that the delivery of a service can be properly assessed, monitored, and managed against these targets.

**Service management**: A set of specialized organizational capabilities for enabling value for customers in the form of services.

**Service offering**: A description of one or more services, designed to address the needs of a target consumer group.
A service offering may include goods, access to resources, and service actions.

**Service owner**: A role that is accountable for the delivery of a specific service.

**Service portfolio**: A complete set of products and services that are managed throughout their lifecycles by an organization.

**Service provider**: A role performed by an organization in a service relationship to provide services to consumers.

**Service provision**: Activities performed by an organization to provide services.
It includes management of resources, configured to deliver the service, access to these resources for users, fulfillment of the agreed service actions, service performance management, and continual improvement.
It may also include the supply of goods.

**Service relationship**: A cooperation between a service provider and service consumer.
Service relationships include service provision, service consumption, and service relationship management.

**Service relationship management**: Joint activities performed by a service provider and a service consumer to ensure continual value co-creation based on agreed and available service offerings.

**Service request**: A request from a user or a user's authorized representative that initiates a service action which has been agreed as a normal part of service delivery.

**Service request management practice**: The practice of supporting the agreed quality of a service by handling all predefined, user-initiated service requests in an effective and user-friendly manner.

**Service validation and testing practice**: The practice of ensuring that new or changed products and services meet defined requirements.

**Service value system** (SVS): A model representing how all the components and activities of an organization work together to facilitate value creation.

**Software development and management practice**: The practice of ensuring that applications meet stakeholder needs in terms of functionality, reliability, maintainability, compliance, and auditability.

**Sourcing**: The activity of planning and obtaining resources from a particular source type, which could be internal or external, centralized or distributed, and open or proprietary.

**Specification**: A documented description of the properties of a product, service, or other configuration item.

**Sponsor**: A person who authorizes budget for service consumption. Can also be used to describe an organization or individual that provides financial or other support for an initiative.

**Stakeholder**: A person or organization that has an interest or involvement in an organization, product, service, practice, or other entity.

**Standard**: A document, established by consensus and approved by a recognized body, which provides for common and repeated use, mandatory requirements, guidelines, or characteristics for its subject.

**Standard change**: A low-risk, pre-authorized change that is well understood and fully documented, and which can be implemented without needing additional authorization.

**Status**: A description of the specific states an entity can have at a given time.

**Strategy management practice**: The practice of formulating the goals of an organization and adopting the courses of action and allocation of resources necessary for achieving those goals.

**Supplier**: A stakeholder responsible for providing services that are used by an organization.

**Supplier management practice**: The practice of ensuring that an organization's suppliers and their performance levels are managed appropriately to support the provision of seamless quality products and services.

**Support team**: A team with the responsibility to maintain normal operations, address users' requests, and resolve incidents and problems related to specified products, services, or other configuration items.

**System**: A combination of interacting elements organized and maintained to achieve one or more stated purposes.

**Systems thinking**: A holistic approach to analysis that focuses on the way that a system's constituent parts work, interrelate, and interact over time, and within the context of other systems.

**Technical debt**: The total rework backlog accumulated by choosing workarounds instead of system solutions that would take longer.

**Test environment**: A controlled environment established to test products, services, and other configuration items.

**Third party**: A stakeholder external to an organization.

**Throughput**: A measure of the amount of work performed by a product, service, or other system over a given period of time.

**Transaction**: A unit of work consisting of an exchange between two or more participants or systems.

**Use case**: A technique using realistic practical scenarios to define functional requirements and to design tests.

**User**: A person who uses services.

**Utility**: The functionality offered by a product or service to meet a particular need.

**Utility requirements:** Functional requirements which have been defined by the customer and are unique to a specific product.

**Validation**: Confirmation that the system, product, service, or other entity meets the agreed specification.

**Value**: The perceived benefits, usefulness, and importance of something.

**Value stream**: A series of steps an organization undertakes to create and deliver products and services to consumers.

**Value streams and processes**: One of the four dimensions of service management.
It defines the activities, workflows, controls, and procedures needed to achieve the agreed objectives.

**Vision**: A defined aspiration of what an organization would like to become in the future.

**Warranty**: Assurance that a product or service will meet agreed requirements.

**Warranty requirements**: Typically non-functional requirements captured as inputs from key stakeholders and other practices.

**Waterfall method**: A development approach that is linear and sequential with distinct objectives for each phase of development.

**Work instruction**: A detailed description to be followed in order to perform an activity.

**Workaround**: A solution that reduces or eliminates the impact of an incident or problem for which a full resolution is not yet available. Some workarounds reduce the likelihood of incidents.

**Workforce and talent management practice**: The practice of ensuring that an organization has the right people with the appropriate skills and knowledge and in the correct roles to support its business objectives.

# Acronyms

| | |
|---|---|
| AI | artificial intelligence |
| BCM | business continuity management |
| BIA | business impact analysis |
| BRM | business relationship manager |
| CI | configuration item |
| CIR | continual improvement register |
| CMDB | configuration management database |
| CMS | configuration management system |
| CSF | critical success factor |
| CTI | computer-telephony integration |
| CX | customer experience |
| G-D | goods-dominant |
| IaaS | infrastructure as a service |
| IoT | Internet of Things |
| IT | information technology |
| ITAM | IT asset management |
| ITIL MP | ITIL Managing Professional |
| ITIL SL | ITIL Strategic Leader |
| ITSM | IT service management |
| IVR | interactive voice-response system |
| KPI | key performance indicator |
| MTBF | mean time between failures |

| MTRS | mean time to restore service |
| MVP | minimum viable product |
| PaaS | platform as a service |
| PESTLE | political, economic, social, technological, legal, environmental |
| RFC | request for change |
| RPA | robotic process automation |
| RPO | recovery point objective |
| RTO | recovery time objective |
| S-D | service-dominant |
| SaaS | software as a service |
| SAM | software asset management |
| SLA | service level agreement |
| SVS | service value system |
| UX | user experience |
| VBF | vital business function |

# References

*A Primer on the T-professional.* Dr. Phil Gardner and Dr. Doug Estry,
    Michigan State University, 2017

*ITIL 4 Foundation, ITIL 4 Edition*, TSO, 2019

*ITIL 4 Foundation Exam Specification*, AXELOS, January 2019

*Service-dominant logic 2025.* Stephen L. Vargo, Robert F. Lusch. Elsevier,
    International Journal of Research in Marketing 34 (2017), 46-67

*Value Proposition Design.* Alexander Osterwalder, Yves Peigneur, Greg
    Bernard, Alan Smith, Wiley & Sons, 2014